DATE DUE

DEC 2 1 2010			
APR 30 2015			
MAY 2 3 2016			

Diseases and Disorders

West Nile Virus

Titles in the Diseases and Disorders series include:

Alzheimer's Disease
Anorexia and Bulimia
Arthritis
Asthma
Attention Deficit Disorder
Autism
Breast Cancer
Cerebral Palsy
Chronic Fatigue Syndrome
Cystic Fibrosis
Diabetes
Down Syndrome
Epilepsy
Hemophilia
Hepatitis
Learning Disabilities
Leukemia
Lyme Disease
Multiple Sclerosis
Phobias
Schizophrenia
Sexually Transmitted Diseases
Sleep Disorders
Smallpox

Diseases and Disorders

West Nile Virus

by Melissa Abramovitz

LUCENT
BOOKS®

THOMSON

━━━━✳━━━━™

GALE

San Diego • Detroit • New York • San Francisco • Cleveland
New Haven, Conn. • Waterville, Maine • London • Munich

LIBRARY OF CONGRESS CATALOGING-IN-PUBLICATION DATA

Abramovitz, Melissa, 1954—
    West Nile virus / by Melissa Abramovitz.
        v. cm. — (Diseases and disorders)
Summary: Explores the history, symptoms, diagnosis, and treatment of West Nile Virus,
reviews ongoing research, and discusses why this mosquito-borne disease is such a
threat to humans and animals.
    ISBN 1-59018-343-6
    1. West Nile fever—Juvenile literature. 2. West Nile virus—Juvenile literature.
    [1. West Nile fever. 2. West Nile virus. 3. Diseases.] I. Title. II. Diseases and disorders
    series.
    RA644 . W47A25 2004
    616.9'25—dc21
                                                                    2003005441

Printed in the United States of America

Table of Contents

Foreword   6

Introduction
    A New Threat in the Western Hemisphere   8

Chapter 1
    What Is West Nile Virus?   13

Chapter 2
    How Is West Nile Virus Spread?   28

Chapter 3
    How Can West Nile Virus Be Prevented?   43

Chapter 4
    Treatment and Living with West Nile Virus   58

Chapter 5
    The Future   70

    Notes   82
    Glossary   84
    Organizations to Contact   86
    For Further Reading   87
    Works Consulted   88
    Index   92
    Picture Credits   96
    About the Author   96

"The Most Difficult Puzzles Ever Devised"

CHARLES BEST, ONE of the pioneers in the search for a cure for diabetes, once explained what it is about medical research that intrigued him so. "It's not just the gratification of knowing one is helping people," he confided, "although that probably is a more heroic and selfless motivation. Those feelings may enter in, but truly, what I find best is the feeling of going toe to toe with nature, of trying to solve the most difficult puzzles ever devised. The answers are there somewhere, those keys that will solve the puzzle and make the patient well. But how will those keys be found?"

Since the dawn of civilization, nothing has so puzzled people—and often frightened them, as well—as the onset of illness in a body or mind that had seemed healthy before. A seizure, the inability of a heart to pump, the sudden deterioration of muscle tone in a small child—being unable to reverse such conditions or even to understand why they occur was unspeakably frustrating to healers. Even before there were names for such conditions, even before they were understood at all, each was a reminder of how complex the human body was, and how vulnerable.

While our grappling with understanding diseases has been frustrating at times, it has also provided some of humankind's most heroic accomplishments. Alexander Fleming's accidental discovery in 1928 of a mold that could be turned into penicillin has resulted in the saving of untold millions of lives. The isolation of the enzyme insulin has reversed what was once a death sentence for anyone with diabetes. There have been great strides in combating conditions for which there is not yet a cure, too. Medicines can help AIDS patients live longer, diagnostic tools such as mammography and ultrasounds can help doctors find tumors while they are treatable, and laser surgery techniques have made the most intricate, minute operations routine.

This "toe-to-toe" competition with diseases and disorders is even more remarkable when seen in a historical continuum. An astonishing amount of progress has been made in a very short time. Just two hundred years ago, the existence of germs as a cause of some diseases was unknown. In fact, it was less than 150 years ago that a British surgeon named Joseph Lister had difficulty persuading his fellow doctors that washing their hands before delivering a baby might increase the chances of a healthy delivery (especially if they had just attended to a diseased patient)!

Each book in Lucent's Diseases and Disorders series explores a disease or disorder and the knowledge that has been accumulated (or discarded) by doctors through the years. Each book also examines the tools used for pinpointing a diagnosis, as well as the various means that are used to treat or cure a disease. Finally, new ideas are presented—techniques or medicines that may be on the horizon.

Frustration and disappointment are still part of medicine, for not every disease or condition can be cured or prevented. But the limitations of knowledge are being pushed outward constantly; the "most difficult puzzles ever devised" are finding challengers every day.

A New Threat in the Western Hemisphere

I N LATE AUGUST of 1999, several physicians in the New York City area notified the New York City Department of Health about eight patients with an unusual type of encephalitis (inflammation of the brain). Doctors known as epidemiologists, who specialize in tracking down the causes of and controlling mysterious illnesses, began looking at what these patients had in common. They found that all eight were previously fairly healthy. The patients ranged in age from fifty-eight to eighty-seven. All had fevers followed by changes in mental function. Seven of the people had severe muscle weakness, which is unusual with encephalitis. Three had symptoms of Guillain-Barré syndrome, a disease characterized by sudden weakness or paralysis of the arms, legs, face, and breathing muscles. Four were paralyzed to the extent that they could not breathe and had to be put on mechanical ventilators.

Tests on the patients' blood and cerebrospinal fluid, the liquid that surrounds the brain and spinal cord, revealed a probable viral infection. Investigators also discovered that all of the people lived within a sixteen-square-mile area in the northern Queens section of New York City. All reported that they had been outdoors near their homes on several recent evenings. Scientists then discovered culex mosquito larvae and breeding sites near each of the patients' homes; this finding offered a valuable clue about where the virus causing the encephalitis came from, because mosquitoes are known carriers of many viruses.

Soon, more doctors began reporting instances of other patients in the area with suspicious symptoms, including fever, encephalitis, meningitis (inflammation of the lining of the brain), headache, stiff neck, rash, weakness, and paralysis. A total of sixty-two people in the New York City area were eventually affected in 1999. Seven died.

When physicians tested the patients' blood and cerebrospinal fluid for viruses commonly transmitted by mosquitoes, they found all had antibodies against Saint Louis encephalitis virus. Antibodies are chemicals produced by the immune system to attack specific antigens, or foreign substances that enter the body. In this case, their presence indicated to experts that Saint Louis encephalitis virus was the culprit. But around this time, public health officials became aware that an unusually large number of wild birds, especially crows, were dying in the area. Several exotic

A pathologist examines a dead crow for West Nile virus. Scientists linked the presence of the virus in birds to the 1999 outbreak of encephalitis in New York.

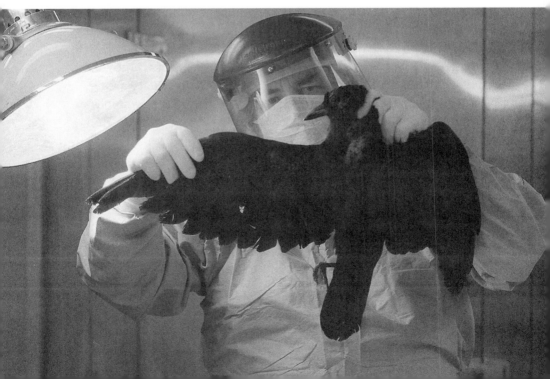

birds in the Bronx and Queens zoos also had succumbed to a mysterious ailment. No one suspected that the bird deaths might be related to the human encephalitis outbreak, but scientists soon made a shocking discovery.

The investigators happened to find evidence of a virus called West Nile virus in brain tissue taken from several species of dead birds, including crows, blue jays, red-tailed hawks, doves, cormorants, gulls, bald eagles, and a Chilean flamingo. This was shocking news because the virus had never before been seen in the Western Hemisphere. It had been documented in Europe, Asia, Africa, the Middle East, and Australia, but never in North or South America.

Wondering whether the bird deaths might be related to the mounting human encephalitis outbreak, public health officials retested the human patients. They discovered, in fact, that the patients were infected with West Nile virus. The preliminary tests that showed the Saint Louis encephalitis antibodies were in error, probably because West Nile virus looks very similar to Saint Louis encephalitis virus in laboratory tests.

Further investigations on more than three hundred thousand mosquitoes showed that eight species were infected with West Nile virus. This evidence helped experts unravel the mystery of how the New York City area patients had become infected with a newly arrived virus. Commented Dr. K.L. Tyler in an article written for the *New England Journal of Medicine*, "The discovery that a cluster of cases of encephalitis in the New York City area in the summer of 1999 was caused by West Nile virus was a masterstroke of medical detection, combining features of a Berton Roueché [popular mystery author] story, a Michael Crichton novel, and Alfred Hitchcock's *The Birds*."[1]

Understanding that the virus could infect birds and mosquitoes was only the first step in answering the question of how West Nile virus suddenly appeared in the United States. Experts believe that it was probably brought over either by birds imported from another country or by infected mosquitoes that invaded imported cargo, but no one is sure of exactly what happened. The outbreak did raise public awareness of the vulnera-

Due to the West Nile virus outbreak, a New York police officer tells visitors to Central Park to vacate the area.

bility of people everywhere to disease-causing bugs that previously were not a problem. Says a report in the *New England Journal of Medicine*:

> The 1999 West Nile virus disease outbreak again proves that, with the growing volume of international travel and commerce, exotic pathogens [disease-causing germs] can move between continents with increasing ease. Physicians, veterinarians, laboratory workers, and public health officials must remain vigilant for unexpected outbreaks of imported disease in the future.[2]

Not only has the West Nile virus outbreak taught public health officials to be alert for new diseases in this country, it has also led to a massive campaign to educate the public about the dangers of the disease and to an elaborate and comprehensive program aimed at preventing and treating further outbreaks. Still, since 1999 the virus has spread throughout the United States and remains a frightening challenge for residents, doctors, and others involved in trying to control this new menace whose invasion continues to intensify.

Chapter 1

What Is West Nile Virus?

VIRUSES ARE SUBMICROSCOPIC organisms that can be seen only with an electron microscope. Their size is measured in nanometers; a nanometer is one billionth of a meter.

As small as they are, viruses are responsible for untold damage and suffering. They can infect many types of plants and animals, producing a wide range of illnesses and even death. They do this by entering a living cell and taking over the cell in order to replicate themselves. In fact, viruses cannot live on their own. They require a host animal or plant in which they can replicate so they can survive, and they must get inside a living cell to begin this process. "A virus relies entirely upon the host cell's ability to create the energy necessary to perform all of the manufacturing processes. Viruses do not come with batteries included,"[3] point out scientists writing for the Virology Down Under website. Thus, the sole purpose of a virus is to enter living cells so it can make more viruses which can then get into more cells and reproduce.

The entrance of a virus into a cell is called a viral infection. It is this infection that can lead to disease. The host plant or animal's body then produces antibodies and other immune chemicals designed to kill the invading virus and rid the body of the infection. The antibodies also kill cells infected by the virus. Eventually either the body is free of the virus, which can no longer survive in the absence of infected cells, or else the virus overpowers the immune system and keeps replicating, leading to death in some instances.

Once a virus is inside a living cell, it uses the cell's machinery and chemicals to produce virus parts, which are assembled into new viruses that then leave the cell and go on to infect other cells. Viruses are made mostly of DNA (deoxyribonucleic acid) or RNA (ribonucleic acid), the fundamental genetic building blocks of living matter. The DNA or RNA is surrounded by an outer shell known as a capsid; this shell is made of protein. Some viruses also have another protein layer inside the capsid known as a core, and some have a fat and protein covering outside the capsid called an envelope. Viruses are classified according to size, shape, presence or absence of an envelope, type of genome (that is, whether the virus contains a single or double strand of DNA or RNA), and other factors.

West Nile Virus

The West Nile virus is classified as a flavivirus, or member of the family known as Flaviviridae. The Latin word *flavus* means "yellow"; the group of viruses is named after one of its best-known

A relative of the virus responsible for yellow fever, the West Nile virus (pictured) causes fever, rash, and central nervous system illnesses.

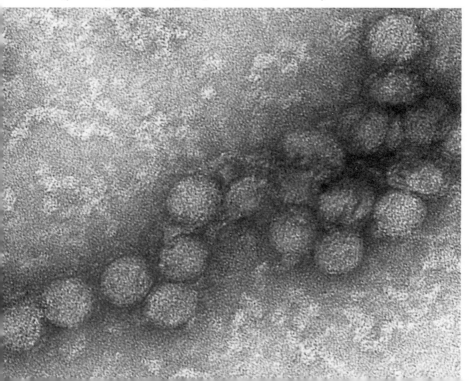

First Isolation of West Nile Virus

In 1937, a group of doctors was studying yellow fever and related pathogens in the West Nile region of Uganda. They took a blood sample from a thirty-seven-year-old woman with a fever, and her blood contained a virus they had never seen before. They named the virus West Nile virus after the area where it was first discovered.

The researchers injected the infected woman's blood into the brains of laboratory mice, and all the mice died after becoming hyperactive, then weak, then falling into a coma. Some of the mice became paralyzed before dying. Subsequent experiments on rhesus monkeys showed the virus caused encephalitis followed by coma and death after it was injected into the brain. The researchers examined the deceased animals' brains and found the brains were swollen and contained lesions and extensive damage to nerve cells. The virus did not seem to affect organs other than the brain.

When the investigators tried giving the virus to rhesus monkeys intravenously rather then directly into the brain, the virus caused only fever and gave the monkeys immunity to its effects. Tests on other species of animals indicated that some became ill and died after being given the virus intravenously or directly into the brain, while others developed only fever and went on to produce antibodies that protected them from illness. Such research with the virus isolated from the Ugandan woman provided scientists important information about it and its effects on the nervous system of both humans and animals.

members, the virus that causes yellow fever. Flaviviruses have a single strand of RNA and an outer envelope, among other characteristics. They range in size from forty to sixty nanometers and can cause many types of ailments including fever, rash, and central nervous system illnesses.

Doctors first identified West Nile virus in the blood of a woman with a high fever in the West Nile province of Uganda, Africa, in 1937. It undoubtedly existed before this time, but no one had ever isolated the virus in a laboratory before this incident.

Soon after doctors identified the West Nile virus, other researchers showed that it was similar to other flaviviruses such as Saint Louis encephalitis virus, Japanese encephalitis virus, and Murray Valley encephalitis virus. All flaviviruses are spread to humans and other animals by mosquitoes or ticks. They are part of a group known as arboviruses, a term that is short for arthropod-borne viruses, because they are transmitted by blood-sucking arthropods.

Outbreaks Since the Virus Was Identified

Since West Nile virus was first identified, health experts have tracked many major outbreaks of disease related to this pathogen in areas where it is endemic (ever present), primarily in the Middle East and Africa. Even when no major outbreaks occur, though, the virus is still active in places like Israel, Egypt, and other Middle Eastern and African locales. Indeed, studies in the 1950s in Egypt found that about 60 percent of the people living along the Nile River had antibodies to West Nile virus in their blood, indicating that they had been infected with the virus at some point. The antibodies that the immune system manufactures to fight infections can remain in the body for long periods of time after the infection is gone, thereby giving the person immunity to the pathogen.

Doctors believe most Egyptians scrutinized in the 1950s studies were exposed to the virus in early childhood during the summer months, when mosquitoes are most active. Most did not develop serious disease and mainly experienced fever and minor aches and pains.

In recent years, notably in 1996 and 1999, experts in places such as Romania, Russia, and Israel have noticed that West Nile virus outbreaks have centered more in urban areas, where the disease was previously not prevalent. The virus has also resulted in large numbers of severe neurological (relating to the nervous system) problems and death when it strikes in places where it is usually uncommon.

The 1999 outbreak in the New York City area, where of course the virus had never been seen before, followed the recent pattern of centering in an urban area and of causing severe neurological disease in many patients. Once the virus arrived in the United States, it showed no inclination to leave and in fact began spreading out of the New York area. By 2000, West Nile virus had affected people in New York, New Jersey, and Connecticut.

Arboviruses

Arboviruses are found throughout the world. They are pathogens that can be spread by bloodsucking arthropods, including mosquitoes, ticks, fleas, lice, and sand flies. West Nile virus is an example of an arbovirus that is spread exclusively by mosquitoes. Most arboviruses are not contagious between humans—that is, they do not spread from one person to another except when directly inoculated into the blood.

More than eighty different arboviruses can cause human illnesses. They typically affect the central nervous system because these viruses have biochemical characteristics that attract them in particular to brain and nerve cells. They can also affect other parts of the body, causing a rash, fever, fatigue, arthritis, or hemorrhaging in some instances.

In addition, by this time veterinarians had identified the virus in many birds, horses, bats, rodents, rabbits, cats, raccoons, and skunks throughout the East Coast region.

By 2001, West Nile virus had infected people and animals in nearly every state in the continental United States. Most of these cases have occurred in Illinois, Louisiana, Michigan, and Ohio. The federal Centers for Disease Control and Prevention (CDC) reports that as of late 2002, there were more than 3,500 people infected with noticeable symptoms and more than 200 West Nile virus–related deaths in this country. Public health officials estimate that there are hundreds more people who do not know they are infected because they never have symptoms.

Varying Degrees of Sickness

According to the CDC, anyone in an area where West Nile virus is present can get infected; however, how sick someone gets depends on several factors. One is age. "All residents of areas where virus activity has been identified are at risk of getting West Nile encephalitis, but persons over 50 years of age have the highest risk of serious disease,"[4] says the CDC. Older people are also at higher risk of developing lasting disability related to the disease and of dying from West Nile virus infection; about 20 percent of older adults die from the disease, whereas only 4 to 13 percent of the rest of the population succumbs.

Another factor that influences how sick an infected individual becomes is the presence of chronic medical conditions such as diabetes, high blood pressure, cancer, or diseases of the immune system. Such individuals are at high risk of getting severely ill and of dying from West Nile virus infection. This is mostly because people with chronic or debilitating diseases are less able to fight off the virus and keep it from overwhelming the immune system.

Recent research suggests that genetics may play a role in determining who gets very sick and who gets a mild form of the disease. Genes are the part of a DNA molecule that transmits hereditary information from parents to offspring. The genes that a person inherits determine the function and operation of each

West Nile Virus in the United States

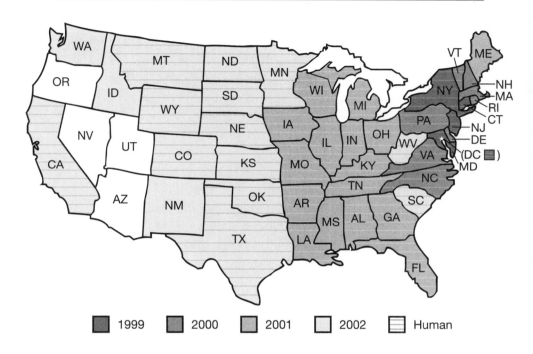

1999 ■ 2000 ■ 2001 ■ 2002 ☐ Human ▤

cell in the body. They play an important role in moderating how an individual responds to various internal and external forces.

Researchers at the Pasteur Institute in Paris, France, tested different strains of laboratory mice to see if genetics might determine which mice were most likely to die from a West Nile virus infection. The investigators found that one strain of mice in particular died within two weeks after becoming infected. They figured out which gene was responsible for this phenomenon and named it the West Nile gene. The scientists discovered that this gene blocks a protein that would usually prevent the virus from reproducing, inducing severe disease. No one has ascertained whether or not a similar genetic flaw is responsible for serious instances of West Nile virus illness in humans, but research is under way to find out.

Other researchers have shown that some strains of mice show no symptoms at all when infected with West Nile virus; it appears

Tracking the Disease

Tracking a disease like West Nile virus involves doctors reporting to public health agencies on instances of infection that are confirmed in a laboratory. Thus, the actual number of cases in a particular area may be under-reported because many people with mild symptoms may never go to see a doctor.

Experts also rely on reports of ill or dead birds and of infected mosquitoes to keep track of where the virus is active. Scientists analyze bird and mosquito tissue samples for evidence of West Nile virus, and if it is found, this information can be used to predict and prepare for new cases of the disease in humans and animals in the area.

that these animals' genes prevent the virus from replicating, thereby preventing serious illness. Again, no one has proven that a similar process exists in humans who do not experience symptoms after being infected with the virus, but scientists believe such factors are likely to play a role in humans as well.

Besides the influence of age, overall health, and genetics, the severity of West Nile virus symptoms can also be affected by how common the virus is to the locale, by the subject's nutritional state, and by how much of the virus enters the nervous system. In places where the virus is endemic, infected persons are likely to experience only mild disease. This is because most people in such areas are exposed to the virus yearly from the time they are very young; thus, they are able to build up resistance. Conversely, in places where it is new or uncommon, as in the United States, it is more likely to result in serious illness because the population has not developed resistance to it. Nutritional state, of course, refers to how well nourished an individual is. In general, people who consume a well-balanced diet have better resistance to infections and to life-threatening complications from these infections. How much of the virus gets into the nervous system depends on individual characteristics like genetics and overall resistance to infection, as well as on the particular strain of the West Nile virus the person contracts.

How virulent, or potent, the strain of the virus is also determines the severity of a person's sickness. Different viral strains result from the virus mutating, or changing its genetic structure; sometimes these mutations can make a virus more or less aggressive, or more or less likely to produce serious illness. Experts have discovered that the strain of West Nile virus involved in the 1999 New York City outbreak was a very aggressive strain, which at least partly explains the large number of affected patients with severe neurological disease.

West Nile Fever and More Serious Illnesses from West Nile Virus

Even with extremely aggressive strains of West Nile virus, public health officials say most infected people do not show any symptoms; in fact, only about 20 percent exhibit signs of the disease. Once someone is infected, the incubation period before they show symptoms, if any, is from three to fifteen days. Experts divide those patients who do show symptoms after the incubation period into two groups. The first group, who are referred to as having West Nile fever, has mild symptoms that resemble influenza, including fever, headache, body aches, and sometimes nausea, vomiting, a rash, and swollen lymph nodes. Symptoms generally last for a few days and disappear with no lasting effects.

The second group of patients with symptoms from West Nile virus become sicker than those with West Nile fever. This category of patients represents about 1 percent of those infected with the virus. They are said to suffer from West Nile encephalitis, West Nile meningitis, or West Nile meningoencephalitis. Encephalitis is an inflammation of the brain; depending on which part of the brain is inflamed, the person will show varying symptoms. For

Symptoms of West Nile Fever

Most people infected with the West Nile virus will not have any type of illness. It is estimated that 20 percent of infected people will develop West Nile fever. Symptoms of West Nile fever include:

• Fever

• Headache

• Body aches

• Skin rash

• Swollen lymph glands

example, if the cerebral cortex, the part of the brain involved mostly in thinking and reasoning, is affected, the individual may exhibit mental confusion, disorientation, and memory loss. These symptoms, of course, would be in addition to the fever, headache, and other typical West Nile symptoms such as lethargy, nausea, vomiting, and body aches. If the cerebellum, a part of the brain involved in movement, is inflamed, the patient is more likely to be unable to walk or to move other muscles in the body. Inflammation in other areas of the brain may produce convulsions, weakness, or even coma.

In rare cases, the inflammation in the brain triggered by West Nile virus infection can lead to a condition called Guillain-Barré syndrome, characterized by sudden weakness or paralysis in the face, arms, legs, and breathing muscles. Guillain-Barré happens when antibodies and white blood cells the body produces in response to an infection damage the cells that protect nerve cells. This disrupts the transmission of nerve signals from one part of the body to another. One patient infected during the August 1999 outbreak in New York City developed Guillain-Barré syndrome and was hospitalized. Extreme weakness, pain, numbness, and tingling in his arms and legs progressed to partial paralysis and the inability to walk. Soon the man needed a mechanical ventilator to breathe. Although these complications are rare in West Nile virus infections, several patients have experienced them during the outbreak in this country. As a result, public health officials recommend that anyone with symptoms of Guillain-Barré syndrome during the late summer or early fall months be tested for West Nile virus.

In contrast to encephalitis, meningitis, the second disorder experienced by many West Nile virus patients, is an inflammation of the meninges—the membrane around the brain and spinal cord. It can produce symptoms of fever, headache, stiff neck, nausea, vomiting, sensitivity to light, and sleepiness. Sometimes seizures are present. It is often difficult for doctors to differentiate meningitis from encephalitis because the symptoms can be very similar, although mental confusion, other changes in thought processes, weakness, and paralysis are generally associated with encephalitis rather than with meningitis. When both the brain and meninges are inflamed, the condition is known as meningoencephalitis. A definitive diagnosis of encephalitis, meningitis, or meningoencephalitis requires laboratory tests that study the cerebrospinal fluid and other tests that take pictures of the brain, in

Symptoms of West Nile Encephalitis and Meningitis

An estimated one in one hundred fifty persons infected with the West Nile virus will develop a more severe form of the disease. The symptoms of severe infection (West Nile encephalitis or meningitis) include:

• Headache	• Coma
• High fever	• Tremors
• Neck stiffness	• Convulsions
• Stupor	• Muscle weakness
• Disorientation	• Paralysis

addition to looking at an individual's symptoms. These tests are performed as part of the diagnostic workup when a patient visits a doctor or is admitted to a hospital with suspicious symptoms.

Diagnosing West Nile Virus

When a patient goes to a doctor or is brought into a hospital, a physician first studies the person's medical history to find out whether other medical problems might explain his or her symptoms. The doctor then orders blood tests to be analyzed in a laboratory. If the doctor suspects West Nile virus, he or she can specifically order antibody, DNA, or virus-culture tests to confirm the diagnosis. If the individual is infected with West Nile virus, the blood sample will probably show a rising level of antibodies to the virus, a positive DNA test for the virus, or a positive culture of the virus grown in a culture dish. A positive culture means that the West Nile virus appears when a sample of the patient's blood is incubated in a laboratory dish used for this purpose.

Persons with neurological symptoms indicating encephalitis, meningitis, or meningoencephalitis will also undergo a spinal tap, also known as a lumbar puncture, to obtain a sample of cerebrospinal fluid. A physician performs a spinal tap by inserting a long, hollow needle between two lower vertebrae and into the spinal column. Then the doctor withdraws a sample of cerebrospinal fluid. If the person has West Nile virus, laboratory DNA and immune-chemical tests will indicate the presence of the virus and an increased white blood cell count in response to the infection.

In addition to the spinal tap, persons with neurological symptoms may be given an electroencephalogram (EEG). Here, electrodes attached to the head and to a machine known as an electroencephalograph record the brain waves on a moving sheet of paper. The test can help doctors determine whether the source of certain neurological symptoms is a seizure disorder or another type of illness.

Brain imaging techniques such as computerized tomography (CT) scans or magnetic resonance imaging (MRI) may also be employed to reveal inflammation and swelling in the brain and

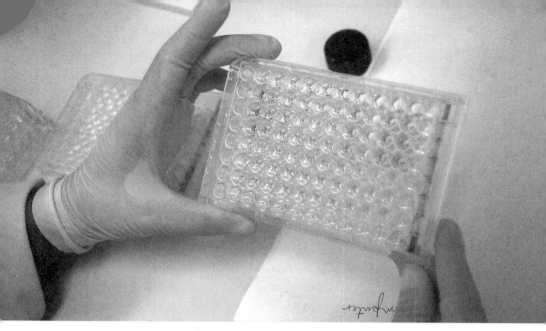

A doctor tests a blood sample for West Nile virus. A positive sample has high levels of antibodies to the virus.

meninges. These diagnostic tools help physicians determine whether a West Nile virus patient has encephalitis or meningitis. CT scans are X rays that produce more-detailed images of internal organs than do traditional X rays. These scans can pinpoint infections or inflammation deep within the brain.

MRI uses a magnetic field and radio waves to create images of the inside of the body. An MRI machine is a large, cylindrical magnetic tube. When a person is placed inside the machine, radio waves produced by a coil in the machine cause the body to emit faint signals. The machine picks up these signals and processes them through a computer that creates corresponding images from the person's insides. Specially trained doctors can then analyze certain body tissues by the electronic characteristics they display. In this manner, a physician can determine whether the individual has encephalitis, meningitis, or other characteristic symptoms of West Nile virus.

A Complicated Process

With the wide variety of symptoms and the similarities among the various classifications of West Nile virus infection, it can be difficult for physicians to differentiate among the subtypes and to actually diagnose the disease at all unless the correct tests are performed. Now that experts are aware of the presence of West Nile virus in the United States, doctors have been alerted to watch for suspicious symptoms and to perform appropriate tests. However, it is still often difficult to decide when one is dealing with West Nile virus as opposed to influenza or to encephalitis or meningitis brought on by other causes.

The fact that West Nile virus looks very similar to other flaviviruses when viewed under an electron microscope and in DNA and immune protein tests also complicates the diagnostic process. This was illustrated in the 1999 New York City–area West Nile virus outbreak in which physicians originally thought the affected patients were suffering from Saint Louis encephalitis virus. However, recent improvements in methods of laboratory identification of West Nile virus have made it easier for experts to pinpoint exactly which pathogen is responsible for a patient's symptoms.

Because Saint Louis encephalitis virus (pictured) looks similar to West Nile virus, physicians mistakenly identified the encephalitis virus as the pathogen responsible for the 1999 outbreak.

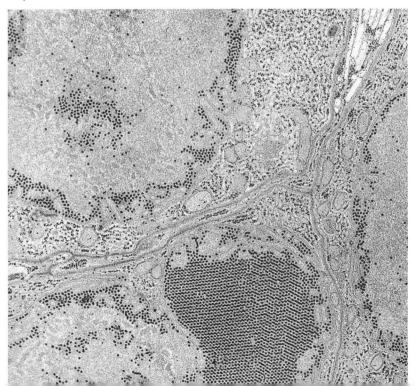

Public health officials have gone to great lengths to educate both doctors and the public about the virus so that it will be considered in diagnosis of anyone with suspicious symptoms, particularly during the summer and early fall months. But in some places with moderate climates where mosquitoes are active year-round, it is possible for people to be infected at any time, so experts emphasize that West Nile should always be considered as a possibility. "Severe neurological disease due to WNV [West Nile virus] infection has occurred in patients of all ages. Year-round transmission is possible in some areas. Therefore WNV should be considered in all persons with unexplained encephalitis and meningitis,"[5] say authorities at the CDC.

After the Diagnosis

Once someone is diagnosed with West Nile virus, the illness is reported to local, state, and federal public health officials as part of a concerted effort to track the spread of the disease throughout the nation. Data on when and where West Nile virus infections occur is then used to track down the immediate causes of the disease in hopes of gaining control over the rapidly spreading menace.

Chapter 2

How Is West Nile Virus Spread?

THERE ARE TWO main types of West Nile virus capable of causing disease. Scientists have identified these two major types, or lineages, of the virus by using sophisticated gene sequencing techniques. These methods involve chemically separating the virus's DNA or RNA strands, the structures which house genes. Once these strands are separated, the genes on them can be mapped and sequenced with the aid of a computer. This identifies where different genes are on the DNA or RNA molecules. Different gene sequences characterize different lineages of a particular virus.

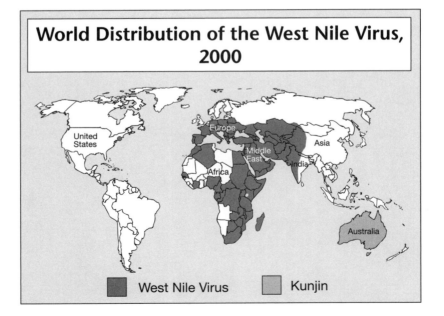

World Distribution of the West Nile Virus, 2000

Investigators have discovered that only one of the two known lineages of West Nile virus causes human West Nile fever and West Nile encephalitis, meningitis, and meningoencephalitis. This group is known as Lineage One. Lineage One virus has been conclusively identified as causing West Nile virus outbreaks in Africa, Europe, Asia, the Middle East, and the United States. The virus grouping can be further broken down into subtypes, or different strains, whose genetic sequence may differ slightly, making these subtypes more or less aggressive or resistant to an immune-system response. One subtype of Lineage One West Nile virus known as Kunjin virus has been identified in cases of disease in Australia.

Lineage Two West Nile viruses are not associated with human disease. This viral group has been found in animals in Africa but does not appear to play a role in causing infections in humans.

Going Places

Although experts are not entirely sure how Lineage One West Nile virus suddenly arrived in the United States in 1999, they do know that birds and mosquitoes are involved in the transmission of this virus to people and other animals. This leads public health authorities to believe that either imported birds or infected mosquito larvae in internationally shipped cargo were responsible for the New York City–area outbreak. They have further narrowed down the strain of the virus that invaded the United States to one that is identical to a strain seen in outbreaks in Romania in 1996 and in Israel in 1998, so it is likely that the causative virus in the United States came from one of these two locations. Scientists at the National Veterinary Sciences Laboratories performed this comparison by sending tissue taken from dead birds found in New York City to the CDC laboratory in Fort Collins, Colorado. There, biologists matched the genetic structure of the West Nile virus found in the bird tissue with samples sent from Romania and Israel.

Birds to Mosquitoes

In addition to matching the genetic structure of these samples to determine the strain of the virus, scientists were able to track the manner in which the virus was then spread from birds to humans and other animals. This has led to an understanding of how West Nile virus causes disease as well as to information about which strain of the virus is responsible for a particular outbreak.

The infection begins in birds, so they are known as the primary host. Scientists performing studies in Egypt between 1952 and 1954 first associated birds with the virus when they found antibodies to West Nile virus in several common species of birds. Later studies showed that human epidemics of West Nile virus followed the illness or death of large numbers of birds, and other research proved that birds are indeed the starting place for the spread of the virus. More than one hundred species of birds have been found to carry West Nile virus, which sometimes kills the bird but often just makes the animal temporarily sick. Studies in the United States since the 1999 outbreak of West Nile virus have shown that the birds that survive the infection are mainly responsible for spreading the virus throughout the nation. "The virus has spread in the United States along the migratory patterns of birds,"[6] say experts at the Mayo Clinic.

There have not been any documented instances of people or other animals contracting West Nile virus directly from an infected bird, however. Although public health officials caution that it is unwise to touch a dead or ill bird for other health reasons, they say it is very unlikely that such an act would result in the transmission of West Nile virus.

While researchers are not sure how birds contract the virus, they do know how the virus is transmitted to other animals and people. Once a bird is infected with the virus, the pathogen can be spread by mosquitoes that bite the infected bird, become infected themselves, and then pass the infection on to another animal or person they later bite. This transmission cycle, like the evidence that birds are the primary hosts for the virus, was first documented in studies in Egypt between 1952 and 1954. At that time, scientists showed that four different species of mosquitoes were capable of transmitting West Nile virus after biting infected birds. Subsequent research has shown that many other types of mosquitoes as well can pass the virus to people and other animals.

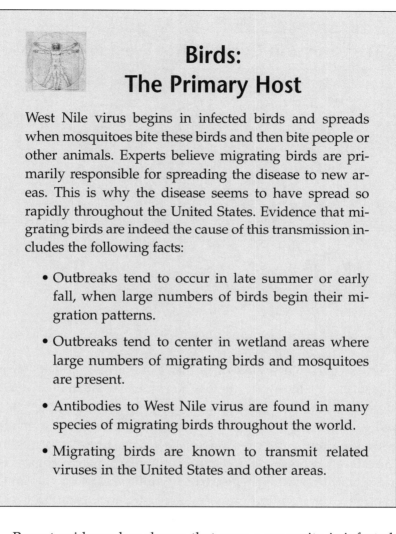

Birds:
The Primary Host

West Nile virus begins in infected birds and spreads when mosquitoes bite these birds and then bite people or other animals. Experts believe migrating birds are primarily responsible for spreading the disease to new areas. This is why the disease seems to have spread so rapidly throughout the United States. Evidence that migrating birds are indeed the cause of this transmission includes the following facts:

- Outbreaks tend to occur in late summer or early fall, when large numbers of birds begin their migration patterns.

- Outbreaks tend to center in wetland areas where large numbers of migrating birds and mosquitoes are present.

- Antibodies to West Nile virus are found in many species of migrating birds throughout the world.

- Migrating birds are known to transmit related viruses in the United States and other areas.

Recent evidence has shown that once a mosquito is infected, the virus does not seem to affect the insect. West Nile virus can survive inside so-called overwintering, or hibernating, mosquitoes that are inactive during the winter months. This is what experts believe happened during the winter of 2000 in New York, following the late summer 1999 outbreak in that area. The infected mosquitoes harbored the virus through that winter and then started infecting people and animals during the summer of 2000 when the mosquitoes became active again.

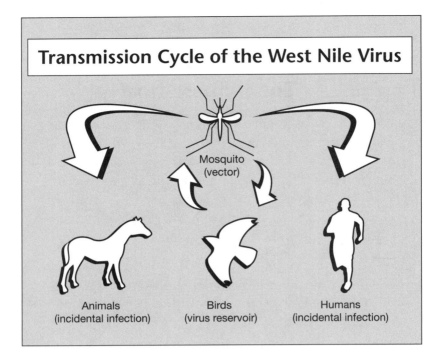

Transmission Cycle of the West Nile Virus

Mosquito
(vector)

Animals
(incidental infection)

Birds
(virus reservoir)

Humans
(incidental infection)

Once a person or animal other than a bird is infected with West Nile virus by a mosquito, there is no evidence that an uninfected mosquito that bites that person or animal can acquire the virus and pass it along to others. Because infected people and animals other than birds and mosquitoes do not usually play a role in spreading West Nile virus, they are known by epidemiologists as incidental hosts. Mosquitoes, which are necessary for transmitting the virus from the primary host to the incidental host, are known as the vector. Thus, the usual cycle of transmission is primary host to vector to incidental host.

How Does the Virus Spread?

After a mosquito bites an infected bird to feed on its blood, it carries West Nile virus in its salivary glands. Then, when it bites a human or another animal to obtain another blood meal, it injects the virus into the person or animal's bloodstream, where it can multiply and cause disease. There is no evidence that parent mosquitoes pass the virus on to their offspring when they lay eggs;

experts believe newly hatched mosquitoes must bite an infected bird to become infected themselves.

Once the virus has multiplied in the bloodstream of a person or animal, it does its major damage by crossing the blood-brain barrier into the central nervous system. The blood-brain barrier is a mechanism present in people and many animals to prevent most toxins and pathogens from moving from the blood into the brain. Biologists believe the blood-brain barrier evolved to protect the body's center of thought, behavior, and automatic activities from being damaged by most poisons and germs in the environment.

However, the blood-brain barrier is selectively permeable, meaning that it is designed to allow some substances to enter the brain. This is necessary so that certain nutrients needed by the brain are permitted to enter. This selective permeability is achieved by means of the tightly packed cells that line the small blood vessels, or capillaries, in the central nervous system. In the rest of the body, these lining cells have a small space between each other to allow substances to move freely between the inside and outside of the capillary. But the tightly packed cells in the

This inflamed cross section of brain tissue shows evidence of West Nile virus. The virus does the most damage to the central nervous system.

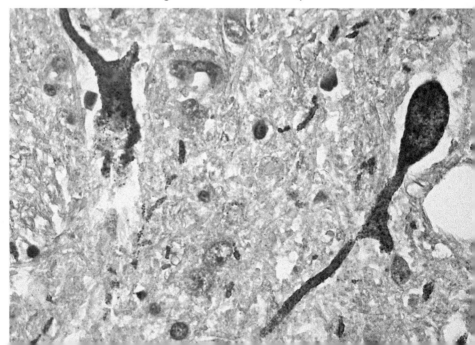

central-nervous-system capillaries allow only certain substances of a small enough size to get through.

Even with the blood-brain barrier, unfortunately, some dangerous pathogens and chemicals are able to get into the central nervous system. West Nile virus is one infectious agent that can get through the barrier. Once inside the brain and spinal cord, it can cause the inflammation and other characteristics typically found in cases of West Nile virus infection. The severity of disease in a particular person or animal is at least partly determined by how much of the virus gets into the central nervous system to reproduce.

More Mosquitoes, More Disease

The chance of being bitten by a mosquito so that West Nile virus gains a foothold in the nervous system is, in turn, determined by the number of infected mosquitoes in a given area. This factor is influenced by several variables. One variable is, of course, the number of infected birds that the mosquitoes can bite to begin the transmission cycle. The more infected birds there are, the more likely it is that many mosquitoes will become infected.

Large numbers of infected birds are commonly found in areas near large rivers. Experts believe that rivers played a role in several recent West Nile virus epidemics. These epidemics all occurred in the late 1990s, one in Romania in 1996, one in Russia in 1999, and the one in New York in 1999. "All three sites were located adjacent to large rivers, presumably providing a favorable wetland habitat for attracting both resident and migratory species of wild birds,"[7] points out an article in the book *West Nile Virus*.

Other environmental factors can increase the number of mosquitoes and therefore increase the probability of being bitten by an infected mosquito. Many experts believe human population growth and its accompanying changes in ecology are largely responsible for the recent heightened incidence of West Nile virus throughout the world. With more people come changes in agriculture and irrigation practices, and this can increase the amount of wet breeding areas and hospitable habitats for mosquitoes. Destruction of forests can lead to further disruptions in the natural balance of animal and insect life.

Another environmental factor that many public health authorities believe has increased the mosquito population is global
warming, the phenomenon in which the entire planet is growing
warmer due to pollution and a host of other contributing conditions. Because mosquitoes thrive best in warm, moist climates,
increases in the temperature or humidity can play a role in
increasing the number of mosquitoes.

Along with global warming, annual fluctuations in temperature and rainfall can influence how many mosquitoes appear in
a given location. Warmer winters in particular allow more mosquitoes in an area to survive, meaning that during the following
summer and fall, there will be more mosquitoes around to breed
and bite. Heavy rains that leave many areas of standing water
can also mean greater than normal mosquito populations. This is
what authorities believe happened during a 1974 epidemic in a
normally dry region of the Republic of South Africa. Unusually
heavy rains that year created fertile breeding grounds for mosquitoes that became infected with West Nile virus. These mosquitoes then passed the virus to more than three thousand
people during the largest West Nile virus epidemic that continent
has ever reported.

Public health experts point out that rainfall is not the only
source of water that can provide mosquito breeding grounds.
Any source of standing water can have the same effect, as shown
by the 1996 West Nile virus outbreak in Bucharest, Romania. Authorities have linked this outbreak to run-down conditions in urban areas where the disease struck. These conditions gave
mosquitoes a place to breed, and the urban setting allowed these
mosquitoes access to plenty of people. As epidemiologists explained in the book *West Nile Virus*:

> During the epidemic investigation in Bucharest, blockhouses
> were commonly found to be in poor general condition, often
> with basements flooded with drinking water or raw sewage.
> Public corridors commonly harbored large resting populations
> of adult *Cx. Pipiens* [a species of mosquito known to transmit
> West Nile virus]. . . . Individual apartments and single family

homes often lacked window and door screens, and those screens that were present were often in disrepair.[8]

Species of Mosquitoes That Transmit West Nile Virus

Experts say that it is not merely the number of mosquitoes in an area that determines the likelihood of someone being bitten and infected with West Nile virus. It also depends on the species of the mosquitoes present. Some species do not seem to carry West Nile virus, while others do carry it and are capable of transmitting it to people and animals. Scientists assess which species are

Mosquito traps enable scientists to monitor and identify mosquito populations. Mosquitoes transmit West Nile virus to people and animals.

Mosquito Traps

There are several types of mosquito traps used to collect mosquitoes for identification and prevalence counts. Light traps are employed most often. These are compact, light-weight, and contain a small motor, fan, and light with a photocell powered by batteries. The photocell turns the light on at dusk and off at daybreak. The light attracts mosquitoes, which are then blown into a collection net or jar by the fan. Related to the light trap is the carbon dioxide–baited light trap, which uses dry ice, or carbon dioxide, placed in an insulated container, to attract the mosquitoes. Carbon dioxide is the gas emitted from the mouth when people and animals exhale; it is this gas that attracts mosquitoes to creatures from which they seek blood.

Gravid or oviposition traps are designed to capture gravid female mosquitoes—those that are ready to deposit their eggs. These traps are made of a base reservoir filled with hay or manure, known to attract these mosquitoes. The reservoir is connected to a suction apparatus that pulls the mosquitoes into a collection carton.

Fay Prince traps are used in the daytime to trap mosquitoes active during these hours. They contain contrasting glossy black and white panels that attract the mosquitoes. These traps also have a container for carbon dioxide and a suction motor to draw the bugs into a collection bag or jar.

Propane-generated carbon dioxide traps use propane gas for power and also convert the propane to carbon dioxide to attract mosquitoes. Some of these traps also emit heat and moisture so mosquitoes think they are landing on a warm-blooded animal. A suction device then draws the bugs into a collection tray.

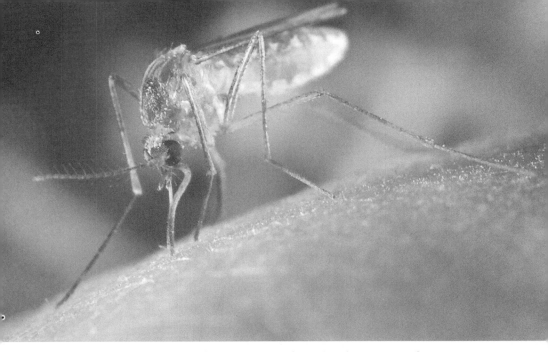

A mosquito bites a human finger. Scientists determine the presence of the West Nile virus in mosquitoes by studying their salivary glands.

or are not capable of carrying the virus by trapping mosquitoes in special mosquito traps and identifying the species. Then, the investigators perform laboratory tests to check for the presence of West Nile virus in the mosquitoes' salivary glands. If the virus is found, the scientists then must determine whether or not the particular mosquito is capable of transmitting the virus to animals or people it bites. Generally, researchers allow these mosquitoes to bite a newborn chicken or other laboratory animal to see whether or not the animal then contracts West Nile virus.

Experts at the University of California, Davis, point out that identifying the species that carry West Nile virus is critical for tracking, predicting, and controlling the spread of the virus throughout the nation: "As WNV expands its range westward across North America, examining the transmission potential of the different mosquito species will help to anticipate patterns of transmission."[9]

Since the 1999 outbreak of West Nile virus in the New York City area, scientists have found more than twenty-five mosquito species that carry and transmit the virus. The vector responsible for causing most cases of the disease is *Culex pipiens*. Other common vec-

tors include *Culex salinarius, Culex restuans, Ochlerotatus ca
Ochlerotatus japonicus, Aedes vexans,* and *Culiseta melanura.*

Other Modes of Transmission

Until very recently, experts believed that the mosquito species capable of spreading West Nile virus was the only mode of transmission from birds to other animals and people. Doctors thought that the virus could not be passed from humans to other humans or from animals to other animals. However, recent occurrences have shown that this is not true; indeed, the virus has been transmitted to people through blood transfusions and organ transplants, through an infected mother's milk to her nursing baby, from a pregnant mother to her unborn child, and to laboratory workers stabbed by needles containing infected tissue.

One instance in which the virus was transmitted via a blood transfusion involved a forty-seven-year-old man in Michigan. Ten days after he received a liver transplant and a blood transfusion, he developed a fever and encephalitis. Tests on his cerebrospinal fluid revealed West Nile virus antibodies. The man recovered, and the infection was traced to the individual who donated the blood to him; the same donor also infected three other blood recipients.

In another recent case, medical investigators identified transplanted organs as the source of West Nile virus infections in four people. All four received organs from an infected donor who died in an automobile accident in Georgia. One patient, who received a kidney transplant, developed a fever, backache, diarrhea, rash, and breathing difficulties two weeks after the procedure. Over the next few days, she experienced a deterioration in her thought processes and required a mechanical ventilator to breathe. She eventually recovered, but laboratory tests showed evidence of West Nile virus infection. A male kidney transplant recipient who developed similar symptoms a few weeks after his transplant was not so fortunate and died from the West Nile virus infection. The other two patients who received organs from the infected donor—a woman who got the liver and a man who received a new heart—also developed symptoms.

Laboratory evidence revealed they had West Nile virus, but they recovered.

Health authorities are taking steps to ensure that this type of transmission does not occur again; however, at this time, donated organs and blood are not being screened for West Nile virus. Experts say the risk of contracting the virus via these routes is extremely small, but they urge caution nonetheless.

Transmission from Mother to Baby

Recent evidence shows that West Nile virus can also be spread from a pregnant woman to her fetus and from a nursing mother to her baby. The pregnant woman, a resident of New York, was hospitalized during the summer of 2002 with fever, headache, vomiting, and back and abdominal pain. Blood tests revealed the presence of West Nile virus. When the baby was born three months later, it had extensive birth defects and its blood had antibodies to West Nile virus, indicating that infection had occurred and was possibly to blame for the birth defects. Doctors say this case illustrates the fact that it is critical for pregnant women to protect themselves against mosquito bites.

A nursing mother in Michigan proved that West Nile virus can be transmitted through breast milk. Shortly after giving birth, the mother contracted West Nile virus from a blood transfusion. Laboratory tests showed evidence of the virus in her breast milk, and her baby's blood tested positive for the virus three weeks later. The baby, however, showed no symptoms of the infection. The American Academy of Pediatrics and the American Academy of Family Physicians issued a statement saying that women who have symptoms of West Nile virus should not stop breast-feeding their infants since the risk of transmission is low.

Danger in the Laboratory

Recent incidents in which laboratory workers contracted West Nile virus after being lacerated with contaminated instruments underscored the importance of caution on the laboratory front, too. In one instance, a microbiologist using a scalpel to remove a dead blue jay's brain cut his thumb with the scalpel. Despite the

A lab worker tests a crow for West Nile virus. Several workers have contracted the virus after cutting themselves with contaminated instruments.

fact that the wound was thoroughly cleaned and bandaged, four days later the microbiologist experienced symptoms of West Nile virus infection, and blood tests revealed the presence of West Nile virus antibodies. In another case, a microbiologist working on mouse brains infected with West Nile virus punctured a finger with a contaminated needle. Again, despite the fact that the wound was cleaned well, the man developed symptoms, and laboratory evidence confirmed that he had West Nile virus. Both microbiologists recovered from the illness, but the CDC issued alerts and new regulations for all laboratories involved in working with the pathogen.

Experts say that these instances of infection through contaminated laboratory instruments, blood transfusions, organ donations, breast milk, and from pregnant mothers to their unborn babies illustrate the fact that under certain conditions, West Nile virus can be transmitted by means other than the usual mosquito-borne route. They emphasize, though, that there is no evidence that the virus can be passed through casual contact or just by being near a person or animal that is infected. All modes of transmission seem to involve direct inoculation into the body, so there does not appear to be any reason for concern over "catching" West Nile virus in the same manner in which colds or flu are caught.

Chapter 3

How Can West Nile Virus Be Prevented?

K NOWLEDGE ABOUT THE factors that cause the spread of West Nile virus has enabled public health agencies to devise methods to prevent the virus from infecting more people and animals. Since the 1999 outbreak of West Nile virus in the United States, health officials on the national, state, and local levels have formulated extensive plans of action to try to contain the current epidemic and to prevent future outbreaks of the disease.

Prior to the appearance of West Nile virus in the United States, public health departments did not have trained personnel who could handle an outbreak of vector-borne disease. But the federal Centers for Disease Control, along with other agencies like the United States Department of Agriculture, formulated lengthy recommendations once the virus posed a widespread threat. They issued these recommendations to state and local jurisdictions to try to help these departments train the necessary people and coordinate an effort to be ready when or if the virus became a local menace. The recommendations included guidance for cooperation and sharing of information between federal, state, and local health departments; vector-control agencies; agriculture departments; and wildlife monitoring facilities. This required a wide range of specialists, including arbovirologists (experts on insect-borne viruses), epidemiologists, laboratory experts, vector-control experts, veterinarians, and physicians, to be educated

West Nile Virus in Horses

According to the United States Department of Agriculture (USDA), horses are infected with West Nile virus more often than any other domestic animal. Some affected horses develop no symptoms, but about one-third of those that become ill die or must be euthanized. Because of this, many veterinarians now recommend that horse owners and breeders have their horses vaccinated against West Nile virus. Although there is no vaccine available for humans yet, in 2001 the USDA authorized use of a new equine vaccine.

Experts suggest that horses be housed in quarters with screens to reduce their exposure to mosquitoes. There are also some insect repellents designed for horses that can be applied to the animals' skin to protect them from getting bitten by mosquitoes.

A veterinarian prepares to vaccinate a horse against the West Nile virus.

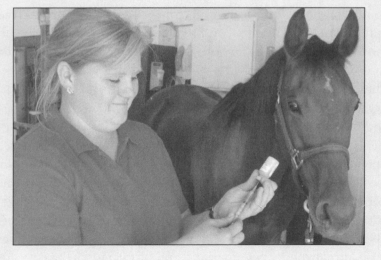

and assigned to programs aimed at controlling th
lenge to public safety.

Surveillance Efforts

The Centers for Disease Control reports that the first step in prevention and control efforts is surveillance of birds, mosquitoes,
and, in some instances, horses. Because horses are commonly bitten by mosquitoes, they can be used as an index of increased
West Nile virus activity. Horse breeders, owners, and veterinarians in certain areas are therefore being encouraged to report any
instances of horses that get sick or die from West Nile virus.

Surveillance of birds consists primarily of monitoring bird
deaths and illness in a particular area and conducting laboratory
tests to find out if West Nile virus is responsible. Residents have
been encouraged to call public health agencies to report such dead
or ill birds, and, in addition, these agencies are actively sending biologists and other experts into the field to search for birds that may
be affected. Scientists then bring dead birds to a laboratory and remove blood or organs such as the brain to test for the presence of
West Nile virus. They also regularly check blood samples from live
chickens and other birds to see if they carry the virus.

If birds in a particular region are infected, biologists use this as
an indication that West Nile virus is active in the area. This information is reported to public health agencies so that the next
step in surveillance efforts—the search for nearby mosquito
breeding grounds—may be initiated.

Once biologists locate mosquitoes, they then determine which
species of these insects are spreading the virus. This is achieved
by trapping mosquitoes and larvae, identifying the species, and
then testing for West Nile virus. The scientists who trap and test
the mosquitoes generally keep track of how many mosquitoes
per thousand show evidence of the virus. This is an efficient
method of detecting increases in virus activity; the tests are usually repeated weekly or monthly, depending on the numbers of
sick or dead birds in an area. If there are large numbers of infected birds, testing on mosquitoes is done more frequently to try
to keep virus outbreaks under control.

In 2000 in the New York City area, for example, scientists collected more than three hundred thousand mosquitoes and tested them for West Nile virus using a technique called polymerase chain reaction. This method of copying DNA enables the investigators to identify a virus present in a sample of living tissue.

Once data shows increases in virus activity, "appropriate and timely response to surveillance data is the key to preventing human and animal disease associated with WN [West Nile] and

Polymerase Chain Reaction

Polymerase chain reaction is a laboratory technique that enables investigators to identify a virus or other living organism by its DNA fingerprints. The procedure was developed in 1985 by chemist Kary Mullis, who received a Nobel Prize for his work. It is sometimes called DNA amplification because it entails replicating a DNA segment to produce a large sample that can easily be analyzed.

The technique begins by immersing DNA in a solution that contains the enzyme DNA polymerase, a series of DNA's chemical building blocks known as nucleotides, and primers that bind with the ends of a DNA segment. The solution is heated to break apart the DNA strands. When it cools, the primers bind to the separated strands and the DNA polymerase builds new strands by joining the primers to the nucleotides. The process is repeated so that billions of copies of a small piece of DNA can be fabricated in several hours. The procedure produces a large enough sample of DNA for scientists to identify the organism from which it came. They have used this technique to identify West Nile virus in blood and tissue samples.

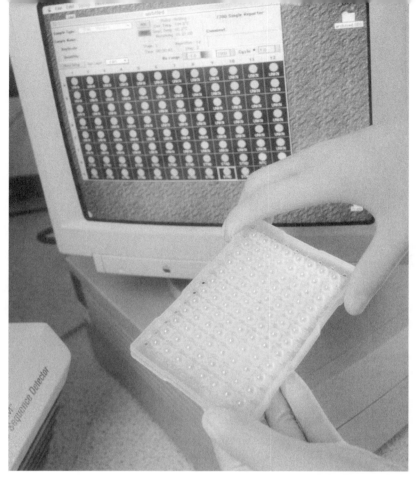

The polymerase chain reaction test copies mosquito DNA to determine whether certain populations carry the West Nile virus.

other arboviruses. That response must be effective mosquito control without delay; if increasing levels of virus activity are detected in the bird or mosquito surveillance systems,"[10] according to the federal Centers for Disease Control.

Mosquito Control

Mosquito control can be accomplished in several different ways. These techniques can focus on any of the four stages of mosquito development. After a female mosquito obtains a blood meal from a person or animal, she lays her eggs in stagnant water or in another wet place. The eggs hatch after about two days, and larvae emerge. The larvae live in water and develop into a third state known as the pupa after one to two weeks. A young mosquito

A farm worker sprays insecticide over an open lawn to control the mosquito population.

lives in the pupa for one to four days. Then a mature mosquito crawls out of the pupa and flies away.

Female mosquitoes can lay eggs every ten to fourteen days during their lifetime, so ongoing efforts at eradication must be targeted toward a rapidly reproducing population of insects. One method of eradication uses mosquito traps containing substances that attract mature mosquitoes. Once the insects are trapped, they are destroyed with poison. Another method involves draining standing water or marshes where mosquito eggs, larvae, and pupae grow. Without water, mosquitoes in these stages of development will die. Still another method of eradication involves biologists placing mosquito-larvae-eating fish such as gambusia into marshes or other wet breeding areas.

The most prevalent method of mosquito control uses insecticides to kill these insects or their larvae. These chemicals can be applied by a licensed contractor either using ground-based trucks or airborne hovercraft. The trucks drop or spray insecticides over a carefully targeted area; hovercraft airplanes are used to spray the substances over larger areas containing mosquito breeding grounds. The insecticides can be in the form of liquids, granules, or solids, depending on the particular situation. If a particular location is windy, for example, exterminators will use granules or solids because they are less likely to blow through the air and expose people and animals to the poison.

Although chemicals used to destroy mosquitoes and their larvae must comply with state and federal safety regulations, they can still be dangerous to humans and animals. For this reason, most experts employ these methods of eradication only when it is absolutely necessary to protect the public's health.

Individual Measures to Prevent Mosquito Bites

These mosquito-control techniques applied by contractors and biologists are only some of the measures that can be taken to prevent mosquito bites. Experts say there are also several things that individuals can do to reduce the number of mosquitoes in an area and to avoid being bitten.

Doctors recommend using insect repellents applied to the skin as the best method of keeping mosquitoes away from people. Studies have shown that repellents containing the compound known as DEET make the skin smell unattractive to the insects and therefore provide the best protection. These repellents achieve this end by blocking smell receptors on the mosquitoes' antennae. Normally, mosquitoes are attracted to people and animals because of odors on the skin and by the smell of carbon dioxide, the gas that comes out of the mouth or nose when the lungs exhale. Female mosquitoes then bite people and animals because a protein in the blood they eat helps develop mosquito eggs. Male mosquitoes do not need this protein, so they do not feed on humans or animals.

In a recent study reported in the *New England Journal of Medicine*, investigators found that products with a 23.8 percent concentration of DEET gave complete protection from mosquito bites for about three hundred minutes, compared with about ninety-five minutes for a soybean-oil-based product, about twenty minutes for a product containing the chemical IR3535, and less than twenty minutes for other plant-based repellents such as citronella, cedar, eucalyptus, peppermint, lemon grass, and geranium oils. The study found that wristbands marketed as insect repellents offered no protection whatsoever. Neither did devices that emit sounds that manufacturers claim are aversive to mosquitoes.

Doctors caution that the true effectiveness of any insect-repellent product varies somewhat according to an individual's skin chem-

A lab worker applies mosquito repellant to his skin. Repellants make human skin smell unattractive to mosquitoes.

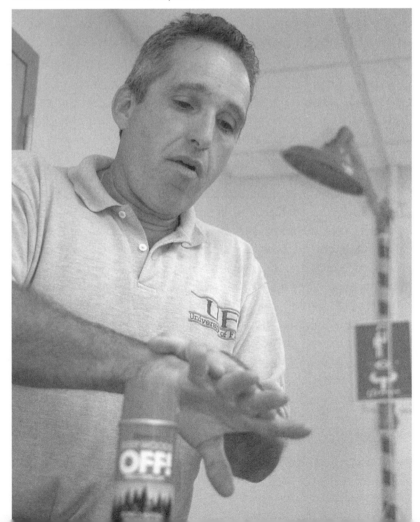

istry, the outside temperature, humidity, wind speed, and how much the person sweats. However, among all the repellents tested in this research, products containing DEET consistently provided more protection than other products.

Many people are worried about applying a dangerous chemical like DEET to the skin, but physicians say that adverse reactions are rare when the substance is used according to package directions. Using too much DEET can be toxic, though, so it is important to use only the recommended amount. This amount depends on the concentration of the compound—for example, a product containing 23.8 percent DEET provides about five hours of protection and should not be reapplied more frequently unless it is washed off by rain, swimming, or perspiration. A product with a 20 percent DEET concentration gives about four hours of protection, a 4.75 percent concentration provides about one and one-half hours of protection, and so on.

Other Precautionary Measures

In addition to wearing insect repellent when mosquitoes are active, experts say there are several other measures people can take to avoid mosquito bites. One is avoiding places where mosquitoes gather, such as areas with stagnant water. Another is staying indoors at dawn, dusk, and early evening when mosquitoes are most likely to bite. A third is not wearing perfumes or lotions that may attract these insects.

Wearing protective clothing can also help. Long pants, long sleeves, shoes, and socks may not be comfortable in the summertime, but are important during times when mosquitoes are out. Clothing can also be sprayed with repellents containing DEET or the chemical permethrin to prevent mosquitoes from biting through clothing. Doctors caution, however, that substances with permethrin should never be sprayed on the skin.

Although public health officials assert that it is critical to take steps to avoid mosquito bites, they also point out that it is not necessary or desirable to panic and stay indoors all day during warm or hot weather. During the 1999 West Nile virus outbreak in the New York City area, many people became alarmed about being outdoors at all, as revealed in an article published by the American Academy of Pediatrics: "When West Nile virus broke out in New York City, callers flooded public health phone lines asking questions such as whether children should play outdoor soccer. Those bitten by mosquitoes rushed to emergency departments. Schools cancelled outdoor field trips."[11] Since West Nile virus is still relatively rare, though, and the chances of catching it from a mosquito bite are not overwhelming, doctors say that extreme measures such as these are not needed. They do emphasize that wearing insect repellent and trying to stay indoors during peak mosquito activity hours are prudent practices that should become a part of everyday life now that the threat of the disease is here. During the month following the New York City outbreak, health officials distributed more than 300,000 cans of DEET-based mosquito repellents through local fire stations and handed out more than 750,000 information leaflets about mosquito protection to help allay some of the widespread panic and to inform the public about mosquito protection practices.

Measures for Protection Around the House

Besides exercising care in protecting peoples' bodies from mosquito bites, public health authorities say there are also things to do around residences or businesses to cut down on mosquito assaults. Draining standing water in the yard is one thing that can reduce the chances of mosquitoes breeding in the vicinity. In addition, the Centers for Disease Control recommends the following:

> At least once or twice a week, empty water from flower pots, pet food and water dishes, bird baths, swimming pool covers, buckets, barrels, and cans. Check for clogged rain gutters and clean them out. Remove discarded tires, and other items that could collect water. Be sure to check for containers or trash in places that may be hard to see, such as under bushes or under your home.[12]

It is also recommended that window and door screens be checked to make sure they are secure and do not have holes. This prevents any mosquitoes from getting indoors. Placing mosquito

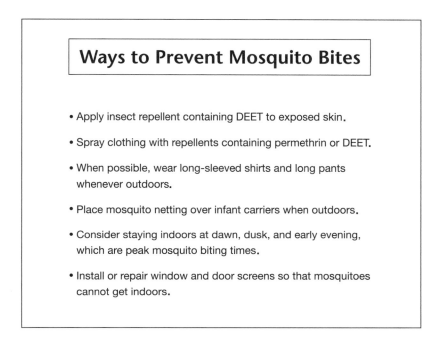

Ways to Prevent Mosquito Bites

• Apply insect repellent containing DEET to exposed skin.

• Spray clothing with repellents containing permethrin or DEET.

• When possible, wear long-sleeved shirts and long pants whenever outdoors.

• Place mosquito netting over infant carriers when outdoors.

• Consider staying indoors at dawn, dusk, and early evening, which are peak mosquito biting times.

• Install or repair window and door screens so that mosquitoes cannot get indoors.

netting over infant carriers or buggies while outdoors is also a prudent practice, and replacing outdoor lights with yellow lights that do not attract bugs is recommended as another method of keeping mosquitoes away.

Preventing the Spread of West Nile Virus Through Transfusions and Organ Donations

Mosquito surveillance and eradication are not the only fronts on which public health experts are focusing their efforts to contain the spread of West Nile virus. Since doctors have discovered that the virus can be transmitted through blood transfusions and organ donations, the U.S. Food and Drug Administration (FDA) has issued guidelines on screening donor applicants to try to prevent the spread of West Nile virus through these avenues. But because only about 20 percent of infected persons show symptoms, authorities acknowledge that until laboratory screening tests are available for widespread use, it will be difficult, if not impossible, to prevent donors who have West Nile virus from donating blood or organs.

Ways to Reduce Mosquito Breeding Areas

• Drain sources of standing water to reduce the number of places mosquitoes can lay their eggs and breed.

• Empty water from flower pots, pet food and water dishes, birdbaths, swimming pool covers, buckets, barrels, and cans.

• Clean out clogged rain gutters.

• Remove discarded tires and other items that could collect water.

• Be sure to check for hidden containers or trash.

Experts now hope to develop laboratory screening tests appropriate for use at blood donation sites in the near future. "Laboratory screening tests to detect donor infections with West Nile virus will be needed if the epidemic persists," states a guidance document issued by the FDA. "Our current thinking is that we would recommend routine use of licensed donor screening tests to detect acute donor infections with West Nile virus once such tests are available. If necessary, we would allow widespread use of appropriate tests under an Investigational New Drug Application."[13] The FDA has the authority to allow new diagnostic medical procedures such as screening tests to be used before they have gone through the normal lengthy testing protocols if they deem it essential in emergencies like this epidemic. The organization has pledged to work with drug companies to make such a screening test available as soon as possible, and several companies are reportedly trying to develop such a test.

Until a screening test is available, the FDA has advised blood banks to turn away potential donors who have a fever or other symptoms indicating that they may have West Nile virus. However, authorities have stated that people who were previously infected but recovered can probably give blood if it has been several months since the infection went away.

In late 2002, the FDA also warned blood banks that blood and blood products frozen for later use should not be used if the blood was taken during a West Nile virus outbreak in a particular area. This meant that blood banks throughout the nation had to quarantine more than thirty thousand pints of plasma, the liquid part of blood routinely frozen for future use. The American Red Cross and America's Blood Centers, the major blood suppliers in the United States, have imposed the quarantine on frozen blood products collected between a week before each state's first case of West Nile virus and a week after the last documented case during a seasonal outbreak.

Special Laboratory Precautions

Since the recent West Nile virus infections of several laboratory workers due to being stabbed with contaminated needles or scalpels, public health officials have also emphasized stringent guidelines for laboratories that handle this pathogen. The U.S. Department of Health and Human Services, the Centers for Disease Control, and the National Institutes of Health are responsible for formulating rules and guidelines for laboratories that use a variety of dangerous pathogens for testing and research. These agencies classify hazardous germs according to the precautions necessary to protect laboratory workers and others from these harmful agents.

Regulations for handling infectious agents are divided into four levels based on how dangerous the pathogen is and on how it can be transmitted to people. Biosafety Level Four (BSL4) regulations are devised for working with the most dangerous pathogens. West Nile virus is classified as a Biosafety Level Three (BSL3) agent because it is considered a serious threat.

Biosafety regulations exist not only to protect laboratory workers but also to ensure that the infectious agent does not leave a laboratory to endanger those outside. This requires that the infectious agent and anything that touches it be confined to a secure place inside the laboratory.

Methods of ensuring safe handling of infectious materials within a confined space are referred to as containment. "The purpose of containment is to reduce or eliminate exposure of laboratory workers, other persons, and the outside environment to potentially hazardous agents . . . the three elements of containment include laboratory practice and technique, safety equipment, and facility design,"[14] explain federal health authorities at the U.S. Department of Health and Human Services, the Centers for Disease Control, and the National Institutes of Health.

Containment regulations for BSL3 agents include comprehensive training for personnel so they are aware of the regulations and have plenty of experience using the required safety equipment and techniques. Such practices also include careful decontamination of anything, including air, that may have touched the

Because West Nile virus is classified as a Biosafety Level Three (BSL3) agent, lab workers must wear protective clothing and handle the virus in an enclosed container.

pathogen; minimal use of needles, scalpels, or other tools that might puncture a worker's skin; not allowing any food or drink in the laboratory area; and not allowing any air to get out of the containment area.

Special equipment required for BSL3 containment includes protective clothing such as disposable masks, gloves, gowns, booties, and eye shields so the virus cannot be touched or inhaled in any manner. Handling of anything that touches the virus must be done in a biological safety cabinet. This is an enclosed container that has its own ventilation system so nothing the pathogen touches can get out. All work inside the safety cabinet is performed through attached arm-length rubber gloves.

Facility design regulations for BSL3 pathogens require that all surfaces be constructed so that they may be decontaminated frequently; the laboratory must have self-closing double doors separating it from outside areas; and the ventilation system must be outfitted so that any air going into the laboratory must not be allowed to get out.

Even with all these precautions, several laboratory workers have been infected with West Nile virus due to unfortunate accidents. Still, authorities hope the stringent regulations will help reduce the chances of infection for anyone who works with the virus and protect everyone outside from possible contamination as well.

The Goals of Prevention

The goal of all these preventive measures, whether in laboratories, blood banks, or in people's backyards, is, of course, to try to control the spread of West Nile virus throughout the United States. Because the disease is so new to this country, data on how well these measures are working is not yet available. However, public health officials hope that educating people about actions to prevent transmission of the virus will soon result in a reduced incidence of infection.

Chapter 4

Treatment and Living with West Nile Virus

ONE REASON THAT health experts emphasize prevention of West Nile virus is that at the present time there is no specific treatment for the illness. That is, there are no known medications or therapies that can eradicate the virus. Antibiotics, used to treat bacterial infections, are ineffective against viruses. Several patients hospitalized with West Nile virus–related fever, chills, body aches, encephalitis, or meningitis have been given antibiotics before doctors knew they had West Nile virus, and these medications did not help the patients' conditions. Doctors have also tried using ribavirin and interferon on patients severely ill with West Nile virus infection. Ribavirin is an antiviral medication that kills West Nile virus in a laboratory test tube and is effective against several other flaviviruses in humans. Interferon is a natural immune-system chemical that can be used to strengthen the immune response to an invading pathogen. However, these medications did not help the patients, and in some instances, they made conditions worse.

Although ribavirin and interferon did not help the West Nile patients to whom they were given, the National Institute of Allergy and Infectious Diseases, which is sponsoring much research aimed at conquering West Nile virus, says that "[These] drugs may be effective against West Nile virus because the infection is typically not chronic and antiviral drugs have been identified to be effective in vitro [in a laboratory test tube] against other flaviviruses."[15] Therefore, experts emphasize that controlled scientific studies and clinical trials on antiviral agents are needed before any conclusions can be reached on whether or not they may be useful in treating West Nile virus. Such studies are also under way on entirely new drugs that might be useful in the battle against the virus.

Clinical Trials and Controlled Studies

Investigations on new drugs to treat West Nile virus begin in a laboratory, where researchers initially test these substances in a test tube or a culture dish to see if they are effective in killing a pathogen. Then compounds that show promise are tested on laboratory animals for safety and effectiveness.

Although interferon is effective in reducing brain inflammation and damage from Saint Louis encephalitis, it has not yet been approved to treat West Nile virus.

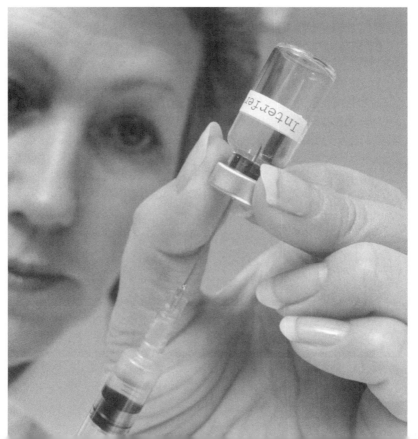

Ribavirin, Interferon, and West Nile Virus

The antiviral drug ribavirin has not yet been proven effective or ineffective against West Nile virus in people. But in a laboratory test tube, high doses of the drug resulted in reduced levels of the genetic material of the virus in infected cells. The drug also decreased cell damage due to West Nile virus infection.

Ribavirin has been used to successfully treat yellow fever and Japanese encephalitis, two diseases caused by flaviviruses related to West Nile virus. For this reason, researchers are hopeful that it will also prove to be effective against West Nile virus when tested in actual patients. It can have serious side effects, such as causing a condition called anemia, so its use must be carefully monitored.

Ribavirin is sometimes used in combination with interferon, a man-made version of one of the body's natural defenses against viruses and other pathogens. In other cases, the two drugs are administered separately. By itself, interferon has been shown to significantly reduce brain inflammation and damage from Saint Louis encephalitis virus in people. Researchers believe it may be useful in combating West Nile virus either separately or in combination with ribavirin. Like ribavirin, though, interferon can have serious side effects, including flulike symptoms and a decrease in infection-fighting blood cells, so it too must be administered very carefully.

Sometimes such laboratory tests are performed on existing drugs, such as ribavirin and interferon, that have proven to be effective against other diseases. These medications have already been marketed for use with other diseases, but before they are approved to treat West Nile virus, they must prove effective against West Nile virus in a test tube.

Once a drug passes these laboratory and animal tests, the researcher can apply to the federal Food and Drug Administration (FDA) to begin clinical trials on humans. These trials are generally sponsored by a research institution such as the National Institutes of Health or by a pharmaceutical company. They are set up at numerous hospitals and clinics throughout the nation. Patients can find out about and enroll in clinical trials through their

A patient receives an injection in a clinical trial to determine the effectiveness of a West Nile virus vaccine.

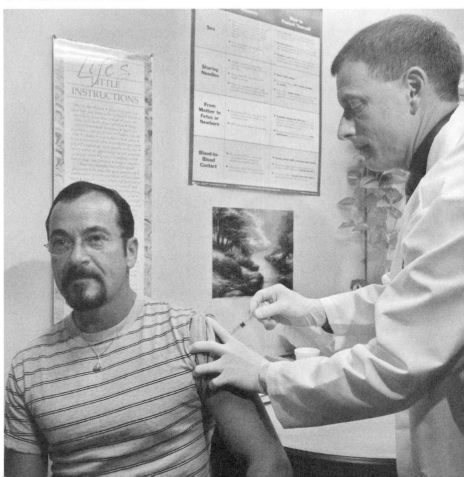

Some Drugs That May Be Effective Against West Nile Virus

Dr. John Morrey and his colleagues at the Utah State University Institute for Antiviral Research have tested many chemical compounds against West Nile virus in the laboratory. Recently they identified six drugs that were effective against the virus in laboratory cultures. The drugs included 6-azauridine, 6-azauridine triacetate, cyclopentenylcytosine, mycophenolic acid, 2-thio-6-azauridine, and pyrazofurin. Each acts in some manner to interfere with the workings of viral cells and therefore renders the virus incapable of causing disease. The researchers indicated that further laboratory testing is needed before any of the drugs can be evaluated as possible treatments in people and animals.

physicians or through sponsoring agencies. All participation is voluntary with the understanding that the experimental drug may or may not help.

Rules and regulations governing clinical trials are developed and enforced by the FDA in the United States and by comparable organizations in other countries. Each clinical trial generally proceeds through three mandatory phases before a drug can be approved for marketing and widespread use.

In the preliminary, or Phase 1, studies, a small group of patients, usually no more than twenty, receives the new drug to determine safe and effective doses and to check for adverse effects. In Phase 2, also known as the pilot phase, a larger group of patients, perhaps as many as one hundred, are given the drug. If the medication does not appear to be beneficial, the clinical trial may be halted and the drug rejected or sent back to the laboratory for improvement. If, on the other hand, the drug gives dramatic results and has few or no adverse effects, the FDA may assign it a so-called fast-track status, where some of the lengthy testing requirements are waived so the drug becomes available sooner to people who need it.

In Phase 3, or the control phase, hundreds or even thousands of patients are enrolled and randomly assigned to either an experimental or a control group. People in the experimental group receive the new drug, but those in the control group are given a placebo, an inactive substance that appears to be authentic. Results from the control group indicate to statisticians whether any positive effects in the study are due to patients' expectation of success rather than to the medicine itself. Patients are not informed which group they are in.

Once Phase 3 is completed in a satisfactory manner, the FDA may approve the new treatment for marketing. Sometimes further studies known as Phase 4 postmarket studies are conducted to learn more about long-term effects or to recheck any questionable data from earlier trials.

Patients who are severely ill with West Nile virus need treatment immediately, so sometimes all these lengthy new-drug testing requirements seem to prevent those who need a drug from receiving it except on an experimental basis. However, the FDA requires such rigorous testing before approving a drug because many new compounds end up causing adverse effects.

Drugs Under Investigation

In addition to beginning controlled clinical studies on existing antiviral drugs against West Nile virus, researchers are experimenting with entirely new chemical compounds to treat the virus. Dr. John Morrey of Utah State University Institute for Antiviral Research in Logan, for example, has developed a technique of screening large numbers of chemical compounds that might be effective. Morrey has already tested hundreds of substances in hopes of finding one that will do well against West Nile virus.

Another area of drug-related research is looking at chemicals that might be able to compensate for a missing protein discovered by investigators at the Pasteur Institute in Paris, France. These researchers have been studying a protein found in some mice that prevents the virus from reproducing inside the brain. In this research, scientists genetically alter a mouse's brain to block this protein, enabling the virus to replicate. A mouse whose protein is blocked tends to die quickly from West Nile virus. Although no one knows whether or not the protein is normally present in humans, experts believe that further knowledge about it could lead to important new treatments. "The most promising thing about this [Pasteur Institute] study is that it could help lead to a drug that would restore the missing protein and give patients protections against replications of the virus,"[16] said Catherine A. Laughlin of the National Institute of Allergy and Infectious Diseases.

Supportive Therapy

Until investigators are able to test and find drugs effective against West Nile virus, the only treatment available is known as supportive therapy. This involves doing what is necessary to control symptoms and make the patient as comfortable as possible, much like influenza or colds are treated. If the person has fever and aches and pains, for example, medications like acetaminophen, which lowers fever and reduces pain, are administered. Patients are advised to drink plenty of fluids and to rest in bed until the body's own immune system can fight off the infection so recovery can begin.

For people who experience more severe illness from West Nile virus infection, supportive therapy may involve more drastic measures such as being hospitalized and receiving intravenous fluid and medications, assistance with breathing, and drugs necessary to prevent secondary infections like pneumonia from starting.

Patients hospitalized with encephalitis, meningitis, or meningoencephalitis often require extensive supportive therapy that includes medications to reduce swelling in the brain, drugs to diminish seizures, sedatives to treat restlessness or agitation, and pain and fever relievers like acetaminophen. Doctors give such

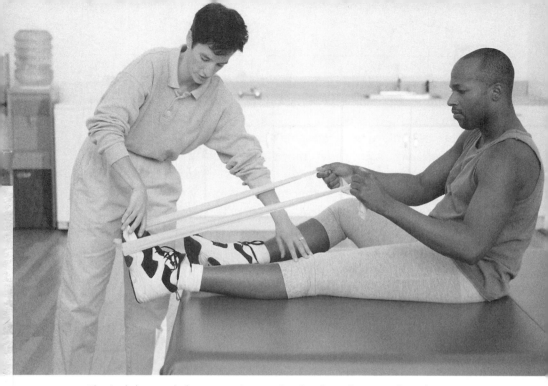

Physical therapy helps to retrain muscles that have been weakened or paralyzed by West Nile virus.

patients intravenous fluids to keep them hydrated and to help flush out the infection. They are also given as much nutrition as they are able to consume or, if unable to eat, are fed through a feeding tube inserted into the stomach.

If encephalitis causes confusion or disorientation, psychiatric care and medications may be needed to treat these symptoms. If paralysis is present, the patient may need physical therapy, occupational therapy, and speech therapy after recovery from the acute phase of the illness. This acute phase can last anywhere from a few weeks to several months. Physical therapy is performed by a licensed physical therapist and involves exercises and stimulation to help retrain muscles that were paralyzed or extremely weakened. Some patients must learn to walk again or to use other muscle groups that were temporarily out of commission. Occupational therapists help people relearn how to perform everyday tasks such as eating, dressing themselves, or bathing that they may have lost the ability to do while extremely ill. Speech therapists may be needed to help a person learn to speak again after being paralyzed if the muscles or brain centers used in speech are affected.

Some patients who develop severe complications from West Nile virus may require even more extensive supportive therapy. One sixty-nine-year-old New York man, for example, was hospitalized with fatigue; poor concentration; and weakness, numbness, and tingling in his arms and legs. This progressed to the point at which he was no longer able to walk. Doctors diagnosed him with Guillain-Barré syndrome, which his physicians believed was triggered by a West Nile virus infection.

The patient was placed in the intensive care unit of the hospital where he was admitted. Soon his weakness increased, and he became unable to breathe. He was placed on a mechanical ventilator and given plasmapheresis treatments. Plasmapheresis is a common method of treating Guillain-Barré syndrome. It consists of replacing the plasma—the liquid portion of blood—intravenously using a sophisticated filtering machine. The goal of this procedure is to free the body of any impurities in the plasma that are causing the Guillain-Barré condition. In this man's case, the plasmapheresis did not seem to help. Doctors administered intravenous gamma globulin, an immune protein, to try to bolster his immune system to fight the infection. This did not seem to help either. The patient developed pneumonia in his lungs, which required treatment with antibiotics. Then he developed blood clots in his legs, so doctors administered blood-thinning medications. After ten weeks in the intensive care unit, his condition stabilized to the point that he was able to be transferred to a nursing home, where he continued to be fed through a stomach tube until he could eat on his own. Although he was gravely ill, this patient did recover and was eventually able to go home.

Recovering from West Nile Virus Infection

Many patients who are severely ill from West Nile virus do not recover and eventually die from the illness. Others get better but suffer permanent impairments of muscle control, memory, speech, vision, hearing, or sensation that must be dealt with for the rest of their lives. Older adults in particular are likelier to die

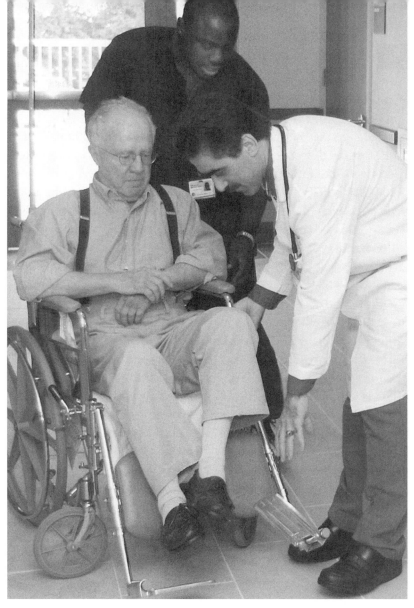

Although older individuals are most likely to die from West Nile virus, those who survive rarely suffer lasting disabilities.

from the disease, but some experts say that those who survive have a good chance of not having lasting disabilities. "In older adults, West Nile virus carries a high death rate—about one in five people—but the outcome is favorable for the survivors,"[17] says Dr. Yitsal N. Berner, a lead researcher in a recent study in Israel. The investigators in this study discovered that 88 percent of the older adult survivors returned to their previous level of functioning after their recovery.

However, another recent study in New York found that 67 percent of the people hospitalized with West Nile virus still reported aftereffects like fatigue as much as one year after leaving the hospital. Fifty percent had ongoing memory loss, 49 percent had difficulty walking, 44 percent had muscle weakness, and 38 percent were depressed after the same length of time. The patients in this study had been hospitalized for two to forty-seven days due to West Nile virus encephalitis, meningitis, or meningoencephalitis. Some were able to go home after being released from the hospital, but some had to be put in long-term care facilities. Even among those patients who were able to go home, several required physical therapy, occupational therapy, and speech therapy.

The differences in findings between the study in Israel and the one in New York may be due to the fact that, in general, people in areas where West Nile virus has been around for a long time do not experience as severe a degree of illness as do those where the virus is newly arrived. This may, in turn, explain why the affected people in Israel, where the virus has been present for many years, did not seem to have as many difficulties living with the aftermath of West Nile virus. In New York, more serious illness in the majority of the patients could then translate into less-complete recoveries.

Recovery and Previous Illness

Another factor that can influence how much effect West Nile virus has on a person's ability to recover and function is the presence of previous illness. Joan, for example, was weakened both by cancer and by cancer treatment when she was bitten by a mosquito and developed West Nile virus. She initially experienced a fever and mental confusion, which progressed to a comatose state. The fifty-five-year-old woman was hospitalized in an intensive care unit, diagnosed with encephalitis, and placed on a ventilator. For more than two months she was unable to talk, move, breathe, or eat, even after emerging from her coma. Finally, after doctors inserted a breathing tube in her neck, she was able to breathe without a ventilator. At a rehabilitation center, she began her recovery, which doctors said would include speech therapy, physical therapy, and occupational therapy. Whether she will ever recover fully is unknown, though chances are that she will experience permanent disability. "Many of these patients who get these serious encephalitis symptoms don't return to their baseline state and many have severe long-term complications,"[18] says Dr. Lyle Petersen, a Centers for Disease Control expert on West Nile virus, in comments about the woman's condition. This is especially true when the patient had a previous illness that weakened him or her before the West Nile virus struck.

Because West Nile virus is still so new in the United States, doctors in this country acknowledge that they lack the firsthand experience to make reliable predictions on whether or not patients will recover fully from the effects of a serious case of the disease. It will take some time to fully assess the long-term effects and the issues that patients affected by these complications will face in living with the aftermath of a West Nile virus infection. Until more studies on West Nile virus patients are completed, experts rely primarily on reports from elsewhere in the world and on knowledge of how people with serious cases of encephalitis or meningitis caused by other infections respond.

Chapter 5

The Future

THE ARRIVAL OF West Nile virus in the United States and the fact that there is currently no treatment to cure the disease have presented a huge challenge for health care experts throughout the country. Since the initial outbreak of the disease in 1999 and since its spread throughout the nation, researchers have been hard at work trying to find out how West Nile virus got here and how to prevent or control future outbreaks.

The federal Centers for Disease Control and the National Institute of Allergy and Infectious Diseases are overseeing a massive effort by a range of scientists to understand the spread of West Nile virus and to develop new methods of treating and preventing the disease. A recent Centers for Disease Control report lists several high priority research projects for the present and future.

One area of investigation involves studies on how and where the disease spreads. This includes assessments of current and future geographic distribution, studying bird migration to determine how this affects the spread of the disease, and pinpointing how West Nile virus got into the United States. It also includes studies on the types of mosquitoes that spread the disease, how to control them, and how pesticides used to control them affect humans and animals. Another avenue of research focuses on identifying risk factors for developing severe illness from West Nile virus, studying the virus itself to find out what makes different strains more or less dangerous, and improving laboratory tests for diagnosing the disease. Other research addresses methods of prevention and treatment including the development of a safe vaccine for humans and animals. Still other investigations look at the long-term effects of West Nile virus on wildlife and on the central nervous system of people and animals.

To achieve these objectives, a variety of specialists are working together. These include arbovirologists; epidemiologists; laboratory technicians; vector-control specialists; wildlife biologists; and federal, state, and local public health and agriculture officials. Hundreds of research projects are under way in several main areas of research.

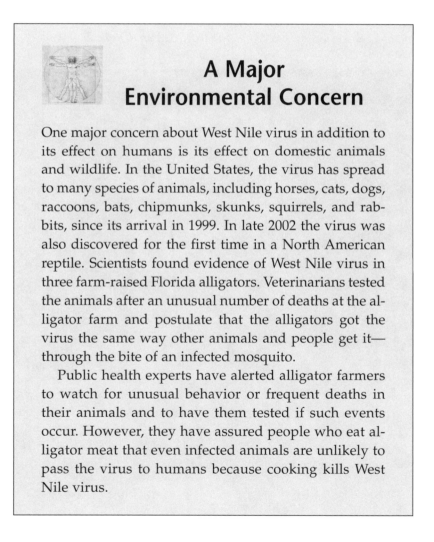

A Major Environmental Concern

One major concern about West Nile virus in addition to its effect on humans is its effect on domestic animals and wildlife. In the United States, the virus has spread to many species of animals, including horses, cats, dogs, raccoons, bats, chipmunks, skunks, squirrels, and rabbits, since its arrival in 1999. In late 2002 the virus was also discovered for the first time in a North American reptile. Scientists found evidence of West Nile virus in three farm-raised Florida alligators. Veterinarians tested the animals after an unusual number of deaths at the alligator farm and postulate that the alligators got the virus the same way other animals and people get it—through the bite of an infected mosquito.

Public health experts have alerted alligator farmers to watch for unusual behavior or frequent deaths in their animals and to have them tested if such events occur. However, they have assured people who eat alligator meat that even infected animals are unlikely to pass the virus to humans because cooking kills West Nile virus.

Research on Transmission and Environmental Factors

Current projects concerning factors that lead to the spread of West Nile virus are important because they contribute to efforts aimed at prevention, control, and treatment of the virus. "The overall objective of this basic research is to develop the knowledge and public health tools needed for the United States to combat West Nile virus,"[19] say research authorities at the National

Dr. Dov Borovsky is renowned for having developed a protein which causes mosquito larvae to starve to death. This helps contain the spread of West Nile virus.

Institute of Allergy and Infectious Diseases, the division of the National Institutes of Health that is overseeing the majority of the West Nile virus research in this country.

One area of research focuses on how West Nile virus came to the United States and on why it seems to be increasing in activity elsewhere in the world. Although experts believe that the virus most likely arrived in this country via an infected bird or mosquito that came on a plane or ship, they are not sure and are searching for clues to find out. This is especially important because other flaviviruses such as dengue virus and Japanese encephalitis virus also seem to be spreading to places where they were previously not found. "The United States is not alone in reporting new or heightened activity in humans and other animals, and incursions of flaviviruses into new areas are likely to continue through increasing global commerce and travel,"[20] say Drs. Lyle R. Petersen and John T. Roehrig of the Centers for Disease Control. If scientists can find out how this is happening, steps can then be taken to control the spread of these pathogens.

Other research on the transmission of West Nile virus focuses on studying migrating birds to see if they will spread the virus into areas of the Western Hemisphere where it has not yet been seen. One study supported by the International Centers for Infectious Disease Research is looking at whether birds that migrate from the New York City area to the Yucatán Peninsula in Mexico will spread the virus to that region of the world. "The emergence of West Nile virus in these new areas, which harbor abundant mosquito populations, could set up conditions for a potentially severe epidemic," state experts at the National Institute of Allergy and Infectious Diseases, who add that "Wild birds and chickens in the Yucatan Peninsula are being examined for evidence of exposure to West Nile virus."[21]

Other researchers investigate new methods of destroying mosquitoes and mosquito larvae as a way of halting the spread of West Nile virus. Dr. Dov Borovsky of the University of Florida's Medical Entomology Laboratory in Vero Beach, for instance, has developed a new protein that causes mosquito larvae to starve to death. He is scheduled to begin testing the substance outside the laboratory in the near future. Mosquito-control experts consider killing mosquito larvae to be the best way of controlling these insects because it is easier to target them during this stage of development before they begin to fly.

The protein is called trypsin modulating oostatic factor, or TMOF. It occurs naturally in mosquito ovaries and serves to stop the development of mosquito eggs. Borovsky and his associates synthesized TMOF in a laboratory, injected it into female mosquitoes, and found that it did not allow the mosquitoes to digest a blood meal, thereby preventing their eggs from growing. The substance had the same effect on mosquito larvae; it literally caused them to starve to death. The researchers hope that TMOF will prove to be an effective way of killing mosquito larvae when applied outside the laboratory as well. They are optimistic that, if effective, it will be an important new method of control, in large part because it does not appear to harm the environment or other animals.

Research on the Virus Itself and How It Causes Illness

One important area of research on West Nile virus is looking at which proteins enable the virus to cause disease. Recent investigations at the University of Pennsylvania School of Medicine in Philadelphia, for instance, have demonstrated that the capsid (the outer protein layer) portion of the virus is responsible for causing inflammation and death in mouse brain cells. If researchers can prove that this element of the virus is primarily responsible for disease symptoms, it may then be possible to target prevention and treatment strategies at this particular protein.

In related research, investigators study how the virus causes an immune response in the central nervous system. One group of researchers at Washington University School of Medicine in Saint Louis, Missouri, found that in mice, antibodies and B cells are critical in this process. B cells are a type of white blood cell important in the body's immune defense system. It appears that they and certain antibodies play a big role in determining which animals are able to fight off a West Nile virus infection and which ones succumb to the disease. The investigators hypothesize that a similar process occurs in humans. Such research can lead to an understanding of new methods of treating the disease. For example, researchers can focus on developing ways of stimulating B cells and certain antibodies if these cells turn out to be the main elements involved in fighting off West Nile virus infections.

Scientists at the National Institute of Allergy and Infectious Diseases study viruses related to West Nile virus to gain a better understanding of immunity to the disease. In hamsters and monkeys it appears that prior infection with the related Japanese encephalitis virus, Saint Louis encephalitis virus, dengue virus, and yellow fever virus gave the animals partial or total immunity to West Nile virus. However, another recent study on humans given Japanese encephalitis or dengue virus vaccines found that these people did not have immunity to West Nile virus. The investigators concluded that immunity to these other viruses does not prevent infection with West Nile virus, at least not in humans; experts say further studies are needed to find out if cross immunity can be achieved only in certain animals.

Research on New Methods of Diagnosis

West Nile virus is currently diagnosed by several laboratory tests that detect immune proteins or genetic material. These tests are difficult and time-consuming to perform, plus they are sometimes unreliable, so doctors are looking for new and improved methods of diagnosing the virus. One of the main research areas focuses on developing diagnostic tests that can rapidly differentiate between different flavivirus infections and that can detect many different strains of West Nile virus.

One group of CDC researchers recently developed a test that accurately detects West Nile virus and distinguishes between it and Saint Louis encephalitis virus in infected mosquitoes and birds. Further testing is being done to see if the test, known as an antigen capture immunoassay, can be used on a widespread basis.

Another group of scientists recently developed a new diagnostic blood test that seems to be more accurate than existing tests. It is called a TaqMan assay. This is a new type of polymerase

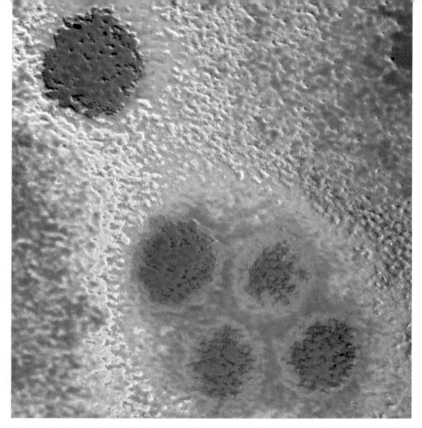

Prior infection with such viruses as the dengue virus (pictured) gives animals partial or total immunity to West Nile virus. Humans infected with the same viruses have no immunity to West Nile virus.

chain reaction test that copies genetic material and scans it with a laser. A TaqMan probe can determine the presence or absence of specific DNA or RNA sequences and thus reveal whether or not a particular virus is present. The procedure got its name because the underlying principle is based on the popular PacMan video game in which the PacMan character must eat tiny blue ghosts in a maze. In the TaqMan test, the enzyme known as Taq DNA polymerase "eats up" the fluorescent tags on the TaqMan probe, thereby releasing color dyes that are attached to the probe. This enables the apparatus to detect a gene sequence.

In an unrelated new development in diagnosis, doctors at Northwestern University in Chicago found that a woman with fever, headache, and fatigue also had tiny lesions in her eyes and complained of seeing dots. She was diagnosed with West Nile virus on the basis of a blood test, and once she recovered, the vision problems went away. The physicians suggested that examining a patient's eyes may provide a diagnostic clue for West Nile virus, but thus far, other experts have not confirmed this finding.

New Drugs to Prevent West Nile Virus

Because there is currently no specific treatment for West Nile virus, development of drugs to prevent the disease is also an area of intense investigation. Such preventive agents are known as vaccines. Experts believe that developing an effective vaccine is critical for several reasons. One, of course, is that it would enable people at high risk for severe disease to avoid being infected. Another reason is that using pesticides to kill mosquitoes is extremely costly, inefficient, and harmful to people and animals as well as to mosquitoes. "The use of pesticides for vector control has raised public concern, with fear of pesticide toxicity being nearly as prevalent as fear of acquiring the disease,"[22] explains an article in *West Nile Virus*.

Researchers are currently exploring several types of vaccines. One is a vaccine developed from a related vaccine for yellow fever. Scientists substituted a surface protein from West Nile virus for a yellow fever virus protein. They are now testing the vaccine in hamsters, mice, monkeys, and horses to see if this vaccine prevents the animals from becoming infected with West Nile virus. Preliminary reports indicate it is quite effective, and Acambis, the Massachusetts company conducting the research with the National Institute of Allergy and Infectious Diseases, plans to begin testing this vaccine on humans sometime in 2003.

Other scientists are investigating whether a vaccine against Japanese encephalitis virus also provides protection against West Nile virus. It appears that this vaccine provides some protection, at least in some animals, but further studies are needed before researchers will know if it is indeed a viable option or if it needs to be altered to provide protection from West Nile virus.

Still another group of researchers at the National Institutes of Health have derived a new vaccine from a dengue virus vaccine, and results so far indicate that it appears to protect laboratory animals from West Nile virus. The scientists, led by Dr. Alexander

Dr. Thomas Monath shows a vial of the vaccine against Japanese encephalitis that his laboratory developed. Some scientists believe that this vaccine may be effective against West Nile virus.

Pletnev, combined a weakened dengue virus with components of West Nile virus to stimulate the immune system to make antibodies against the West Nile virus. Further tests are ongoing before this vaccine can be tested on humans.

DNA vaccines are a relatively new type of vaccine that other researchers are working on. DNA vaccines contain the genetic material of the virus being targeted plus a substance known as a promoter. The promoter helps the gene get into the cells of the animal being immunized. Experts say this type of vaccine is potentially more effective than others because the DNA can be manipulated to elicit the most favorable immune response. This allows more control over any adverse effects and is more likely to produce the desired effect, immunity. Thus far, scientists have shown that a West Nile virus DNA vaccine is effective in mice and horses; further studies will be done to test for safety and effectiveness before this kind of vaccine is given to humans.

Bioterrorism

One additional issue that health officials dealing with West Nile virus are faced with in the present and future is related to the threat of bioterrorism. This is a problem in which terrorists use biological agents such as viruses or bacteria to make large numbers of people ill. It has been suggested that the incursion of West Nile virus into the United States was related to an act of bioterrorism, but CDC officials say that there is no evidence whatsoever that this is the case. These experts also do not consider West Nile virus a likely possibility to be used as an agent of bioterrorism, mostly because it is not easily spread through the air or through casual contact as are other pathogens more likely to be thus employed. However, the West Nile virus epidemic has served as a test of public health agencies' preparedness for such an attack, and lessons learned from the outbreak are being applied to emergency planning for all sorts of emergencies including bioterrorism from a variety of infectious agents. Emergency medicine authorities say in a recent article in the *American Journal of Emergency Medicine*:

> Preparedness for bioterrorism poses unique challenges. In the event of a biological attack, the hospital infection control staff and administration must already have in place the means to communicate with local and state public health agencies, the Centers For Disease Control and Prevention (CDC), local law enforcement agencies, and the Federal Bureau of Investigation (FBI). . . . Most hospitals are ill equipped to deal with a catastrophic event caused by WMD (weapons of mass destruction).[23]

The Challenge for the Future: A Rapidly Spreading Menace

West Nile virus has gone from being unknown in the United States prior to 1999 to the following number of cases, state by state, in 2002. Experts believe that bird migration patterns and the prevalence of mosquito breeding grounds influence which areas experience the most cases of the disease.

Alabama	43	Missouri	128
Arkansas	43	Montana	1
California	1	Nebraska	112
Colorado	13	New Jersey	23
Connecticut	17	New York	82
Delaware	1	North Carolina	2
District of Columbia	33	North Dakota	17
Florida	28	Ohio	442
Georgia	43	Oklahoma	19
Illinois	835	Pennsylvania	60
Indiana	287	Rhode Island	1
Iowa	54	South Carolina	1
Kansas	22	South Dakota	37
Kentucky	75	Tennessee	56
Louisiana	330	Texas	189
Maryland	33	Vermont	1
Massachusetts	23	Virginia	29
Michigan	528	West Virginia	2
Minnesota	48	Wisconsin	47
Mississippi	186	Wyoming	1

Health experts say that hospital emergency rooms must quickly develop specific plans for dealing with outbreaks of diseases like West Nile virus to prevent widespread panic and death.

Priorities in the Battle Against West Nile Virus

In short, public health officials see it as a priority for the present and future to stop the spread of West Nile virus through whatever routes of transmission the virus takes, be those routes blood transfusions, organ donations, laboratory accidents, or infected birds and mosquitoes. Since the virus burst on the scene in New York City in 1999, it has surprised experts with the speed and intensity with which it has spread across the United States. Halting this spread and developing methods of treatment are extremely high priorities for officials who realize that West Nile virus is a menace that can do a great deal of damage to both humans and animals. Said New York State Commissioner of Health Antonia C. Novello at a recent conference on the subject, "One thing we have learned from the West Nile virus is that it can be anywhere, and so we must be prepared for anything."[24]

Notes

Introduction: A New Threat in the Western Hemisphere

1. K.L. Tyler, M.D., "West Nile Virus Encephalitis in America," *New England Journal of Medicine*, June 14, 2001, p. 1858.
2. Denis Nash, Ph.D., et al., "The Outbreak of West Nile Virus Infection in the New York City Area in 1999," *New England Journal of Medicine*, June 14, 2001, p. 1814.

Chapter 1: What Is West Nile Virus?

3. Virology Down Under, "Are Viruses Alive?" www.uq.edu.
4. Centers for Disease Control, "Who's at Risk for West Nile Virus?" www.cdc.gov.
5. Centers for Disease Control, "Fact Sheet: West Nile Virus (WNV) Infection: Information for Clinicians," www.cdc.gov.

Chapter 2: How Is West Nile Virus Spread?

6. Mayo Clinic.com, "West Nile Virus," www.mayoclinic.com.
7. Quoted in Dennis J. White and Dale L. Morse, eds., *West Nile Virus*, New York: New York Academy of Sciences, 2001, p. 33.
8. Quoted in White and Morse, *West Nile Virus*, p. 97.
9. Laura B. Goddard et al., "Vector Competence of California Mosquitoes for West Nile Virus," *Emerging Infectious Diseases*, December 2002, p. 8.

Chapter 3: How Can West Nile Virus Be Prevented?

10. Centers for Disease Control and Prevention, "Epidemic/ Enzootic West Nile Virus in the United States: Revised Guidelines for Surveillance, Prevention, and Control," April 2001, p. 7.

11. Kristy Kennedy, correspondent, *American Academy of Pediatrics News,* "Calming West Nile Fears," www.aap.org.

12. Centers for Disease Control, "Prevention," www.cdc.gov.

13. Quoted in Reuters News Service, "FDA Offers Guidance to Blood Centers on West Nile," November 29, 2002. www.nlm.nih.gov.

14. National Institutes of Health, "Biosafety in Microbiological and Biomedical Laboratories," http://bmbl.od.nih.gov.

Chapter 4: Treatment and Living with West Nile Virus

15. National Institute of Allergy and Infectious Diseases, "Research on West Nile Virus," www.niaid.nih.gov

16. Quoted in "Gene May Explain Why Some Barely Sicken, Others Die," *Houston Chronicle,* August 19, 2002. www.chron.com.

17. Quoted in *Reuters Health,* "West Nile Virus Survivors Fare Well After Illness," December 6, 2002. www.nlm.nih.gov.

18. Quoted in Avram Goldstein, "A Smile, a Hello, a Sense of Hope," *Washington Post,* October 7, 2002, p. B01.

Chapter 5: The Future

19. National Institute of Allergy and Infectious Diseases, "Research on West Nile Virus," www.niaid.nih.gov.

20. Lyle R. Petersen and John T. Roehrig, "West Nile Virus: A Reemerging Global Pathogen," *Emerging Infectious Diseases,* July–August 2001. www.cdc.gov.

21. National Institute of Allergy and Infectious Diseases, "Research on West Nile Virus," www.niaid.nih.gov.

22. Quoted in White and Morse, *West Nile Virus,* p. 3.

23. R.S. Crupi et al., "Meeting the Challenge of Bioterrorism: Lessons Learned from West Nile Virus and Anthrax," *American Journal of Emergency Medicine,* January 21, 2003, p. 77.

24. Quoted in White and Morse, *West Nile Virus,* p. xiii.

Glossary

antibodies: Chemicals produced by the immune system in response to a foreign substance, or antigen.

arbovirus: A virus spread by an arthropod, most commonly by bloodsucking insects.

blood-brain barrier: A biological mechanism that prevents most toxins and pathogens from crossing into the brain from the blood.

blood transfusion: A procedure in which a person who needs blood receives blood from a donor.

cerebrospinal fluid: The liquid that surrounds the brain and spinal cord.

encephalitis: Inflammation of the brain.

epidemic: A widespread outbreak of disease.

epidemiologist: Doctor who specializes in tracking down causes and incidence of infectious diseases.

flavivirus: A type of virus that is transmitted by mosquitoes or ticks.

gene: The basic unit of hereditary information in a cell.

host: Animal that carries an infectious disease.

incubation period: The time between infection and evident symptoms.

intravenous: Into a vein.

meningitis: Inflammation of the meninges, the lining of the brain and spinal cord.

meningoencephalitis: Inflammation of the brain and the meninges.

neurological: Concerning the nervous system.

pathogen: Agent that causes disease.

vaccine: A drug given to stimulate immunity against a disease.

vector: An agent such as a mosquito that transmits a pathogen from primary host to incidental host.

ventilator: A machine that breathes for someone who is unable to breathe; also called a respirator.

virus: A microorganism that replicates itself within the cells of a living host.

Organizations to Contact

**Centers for Disease Control,
National Center for Infectious Diseases**

PO Box 2087
Fort Collins, CO 80522
(888) 232-3228
www.cdc.gov

Provides comprehensive information on all aspects of West Nile virus.

**National Institute of Allergy and Infectious Diseases,
National Institutes of Health Office of Communications
and Public Liaison**

Bethesda, MD 20892
(301) 496-5717
www.niaid.nih.gov

Good information on all aspects of West Nile virus, especially research.

For Further Reading

Centers for Disease Control, "The Buzz-z-z-z On West Nile Virus," www.bam.gov. Fun kids' website about West Nile virus.

Teens Health, "Should I Worry About West Nile Virus?" http://kidshealth.org. Fun and informative teen website.

Works Consulted

Books

W. Michael Scheld, William A. Craig, and James M. Hughes, eds., *Emerging Infections*, Washington, DC: ASM Press, 2001. Technical book; one chapter on West Nile virus.

Dennis J. White and Dale L. Morse, eds., *West Nile Virus*, New York: New York Academy of Sciences, 2001. Comprehensive, highly technical overview of West Nile virus.

Periodicals

S. Ahmed, M.D., et al., "Guillain-Barré Syndrome: An Unusual Presentation of West Nile Virus Infection," *Neurology*, vol. 55, 2000, pp. 144–46.

R.S. Crupi et al., "Meeting the Challenge of Bioterrorism: Lessons Learned from West Nile Virus and Anthrax," *American Journal of Emergency Medicine*, January 21, 2003, pp. 77–79.

Mark S. Fradin, M.D., and John F. Day, Ph.D., "Comparative Efficacy of Insect Repellents Against Mosquito Bites," *New England Journal of Medicine*, July 4, 2002, pp. 13–18.

"Gene May Explain Why Some Barely Sicken, Others Die," *Houston Chronicle*, August 19, 2002. www.chron.com.

Michael Giladi et al., "West Nile Encephalitis in Israel, 1999: The New York Connection," *Emerging Infectious Diseases*, July–August 2001. www.cdc.gov.

Laura B. Goddard et al., "Vector Competence of California Mosquitoes for West Nile Virus," *Emerging Infectious Diseases*, December 2002, p. 8.

Avram Goldstein, "A Smile, a Hello, a Sense of Hope," *Washington Post*, October 7, 2002, p. B01.

Z. Hubalek and J. Halouzka, "West Nile Fever—A Reemerging Mosquito-Borne Viral Disease in Europe," *Emerging Infectious Diseases*, September–October 1999, pp. 643–650.

R.S. Lanciotti et al., "Origin of the West Nile Virus Responsible for an Outbreak of Encephalitis in the Northeastern United States," *Science*, vol. 286, 1999, pp. 2333–37.

Luis Monteagudo Jr., "County Unveils Its Tools to Fight West Nile," *San Diego Union-Tribune*, November 8, 2002.

J.D. Morrey et al., "Identification of Active Compounds Against a New York Isolate of West Nile Virus," *Antiviral Research*, vol. 55, 2002, pp. 107–116.

Denis Nash, Ph.D., et al., "The Outbreak of West Nile Virus Infection in the New York City Area in 1999," *New England Journal of Medicine*, June 14, 2001, pp. 1807–1814.

Lyle R. Petersen, M.D., MPH, and Anthony A. Martin, M.D., MPH, "West Nile Virus: A Primer for the Clinician," *Annals of Internal Medicine*, August 6, 2002, pp. 173–179.

Lyle R. Petersen and John T. Roehrig, "West Nile Virus: A Reemerging Global Pathogen," *Emerging Infectious Diseases*, July–August 2001. www.cdc.gov.

"Two Viruses Team Up in West Nile Vaccine," *NIAID News*, March 4, 2002.

K.L. Tyler, M.D., "West Nile Virus Encephalitis in America," *New England Journal of Medicine*, June 14, 2001, pp. 1858–1859.

Dennis J. White et al., "Mosquito Surveillance and Polymerase Chain Reaction Detection of West Nile Virus, New York State," *Emerging Infectious Diseases*, July–August 2001. www. cdc.gov.

Government Publication

Centers for Disease Control and Prevention, "Epidemic/ Enzootic West Nile Virus in the United States: Revised Guidelines for Surveillance, Prevention, and Control," April 2001.

Internet Sources

Associated Press, "Second Florida Transplant Patient Has West Nile," NBC Net, September 5, 2002. www.nbc6.net.

Centers for Disease Control, "About the Virus, the Disease, and Its Spread," www.cdc.gov.

Centers for Disease Control, "Background: The Virus' History and Distribution," www.cdc.gov.

Centers for Disease Control, "Fact Sheet: West Nile Virus (WNV) Infection: Information For Clinicians," www.cdc.gov.

Centers for Disease Control, "Laboratory-Acquired West Nile Virus Infections—United States 2002," www.cdc.gov.

Centers for Disease Control, "Prevention," www.cdc.gov.

Centers for Disease Control, "Prevention: Avoid Mosquito Bites to Avoid Infection," www.cdc.gov.

Centers for Disease Control, "Update: Investigations of West Nile Virus Infections in Recipients of Organ Transplantation and Blood Transfusion—Michigan 2002," www.cdc.gov.

Centers for Disease Control, "Who's at Risk for West Nile Virus?" www.cdc.gov.

Kristy Kennedy, correspondent, *American Association of Pediatrics News,* "Calming West Nile Fears," www.aap.org.

Mayo Clinic.com, "West Nile Virus," www.mayoclinic.com.

National Institute of Allergy and Infectious Diseases, "Research on West Nile Virus," www.niaid.nih.gov.

National Institute of Allergy and Infectious Diseases, "Testimony Before the Senate Committee on Health, Education, Labor, and Pensions; Senate Committee on Governmental Affairs, Subcommittee on Oversight of Government, Management Restructuring and the District of Columbia," Wednesday, September 24, 2002. www.niaid.nih.gov.

National Institutes of Health, "Biosafety in Microbiological and Biomedical Laboratories," http://bmbl.od.nih.gov.

Lauran Neergaard, "30,000 Pints of Plasma Quarantined," December 12, 2002. www.nlm.nih.gov.

Reuters Health, "FDA Offers Guidance to Blood Centers on West Nile," November 29, 2002. www.nlm.nih.gov.

Reuters Health, "West Nile Survivors Fare Well After Illness," December 6, 2002. www.nlm.nih.gov.

Lisa Richwine, "FDA Officials Urge West Nile Blood Test Development," www.nlm.nih.gov.

Jane Sutton, "West Nile Virus Found in Florida Alligators," November 13, 2002. www.nlm.nih.gov.

Virology Down Under, "Are Viruses Alive?" www.uq.edu.

Index

Acambis (company), 77
acetaminophen, 64
Aedes vexans (mosquito species), 39
Africa, 16, 29
age factors, 18, 66–68
Alabama, 80
alligators, 71
American Journal of Emergency Medicine, 79
animals
    impact of West Nile virus on, 71
    New York City (1999) outbreak and, 18
    see also specific animals
antibiotics, 58
antibodies, 9, 13, 16
antiviral medication, 58
arboviruses (arthropod-borne viruses), 16, 17
Arkansas, 80
Asia, 29
Australia, 29

bats, 18
Berner, Yitsal N., 67
biosafety regulations, 55–57
bioterrorism, 79, 81
birds
    deaths of, 9–10
    number of infected, influence of, 34
    research on, 73
    role of, in transmission cycle, 29–30, 31
    surveillance of, 45
blood-brain barrier, 33–34
blood tests, 75
blood transfusions, 39, 53
Borovsky, Dov, 73–74
brain, 21–22, 33–34
breastfeeding, 39
Bucharest outbreak (1996), 35–36

California, 80
carbon dioxide–baited light trap (mosquito), 37
cats, 18
Centers for Disease Control and Prevention (CDC)
    on bioterrorism, 79
    guidelines by, 43, 55
    reports of, on West Nile virus in United States, 18
    research projects and, 70
clinical trials of drugs, 61–63
Colorado, 80
Connecticut, 17, 80
crows, 9–10
CT scans, 24–25
Culex pipiens (mosquito species), 38
Culex restuans (mosquito species), 39
Culex salinarius (mosquito species), 39
Culiseta melanura (mosquito species), 39

deaths, 18, 66–67
DEET (repellent), 49–50, 51
Delaware, 80
dengue virus, 73, 75
Department of Agriculture, 43, 44
Department of Health and Human Services, 55
District of Columbia, 80
DNA (deoxyribonucleic acid), 14, 28
    amplification, 46
    vaccines, 78–79
donor screening tests, 54
drug treatment. *See* treatment, drug

Egypt, 16
elderly, the, 18, 66–68
electroencephalogram (EEG), 24
encephalitis, 8–9, 21–23, 64–65
environmental concerns, 34–36, 71

epidemiologists, 8
Europe, 29
exotic birds, 9–10

Fay Prince traps (mosquito), 37
FDA (Food and Drug
    Administration), 53, 54–55, 61, 62
flaviviruses, 14, 16, 73
Florida, 80
forests, destruction of, 34

gene sequencing techniques, 28–29
genetics, 18–20
Georgia, 80
global warming, 35
gravid traps (mosquito), 37
Guillain-Barré syndrome, 8, 22–23,
    66

horses, 18, 44, 45

Illinois, 18, 80
immunity, 75
incidental hosts, 32
Indiana, 80
infants, 40
infected people
    central nervous system of, 33–34
    deaths of, 66–67
    factors influencing degrees of
        sickness in, 18–21
    not showing symptoms, 21
    recovery of, 67–69
    spread of virus into, by birds, 30,
        32
    tests on, 8, 10
    see also treatment
insecticides, 48–49
insect repellents, 49–51
interferon, 58, 60
International Centers for Infectious
    Disease Research, 73
investigations. *See* research
Iowa, 80
Israel, 16, 17, 29

Japanese encephalitis virus, 16, 73, 75

Kansas, 80
Kentucky, 80

laboratory work(ers), 39, 40–42,
    55–57
Laughline, Catherine A., 64
light traps (mosquito), 37
Lineage One West Nile Virus, 29

Lineage Two West Nile Virus, 29
Louisiana, 18, 80
lumbar puncture, 24

Maryland, 80
Massachusetts, 80
medical conditions and illnesses, 18,
    68-69
medications. *See* treatment, drug
meningitis, 21, 23, 64
meningoencephalitis, 21, 23, 64
Michigan, 18, 80
Middle East, 16, 29
Minnesota, 80
Mississippi, 80
Missouri, 80
Montana, 80
Morrey, John, 62
mosquitoes
    controlling reproduction of, 47–49
    differences in species of, 36, 38–39
    environmental factors increasing
        probability of being bitten by,
        34–35
    harboring virus throughout
        winter, 31
    passing virus into offspring, 32–33
    preventing bites by, 49–51, 52–53
    reducing breeding areas for, 52, 54
    research on control of, 73–74
    role of, in West Nile Virus
        transmission, 30, 32
    surveillance of, 45–47
mosquito traps, 37
mothers, transmission from nursing
    or pregnant, 40
MRI (magnetic resonance imaging),
    24–25
Mullis, Kary, 46
Murray Valley encephalitis, 16

National Institute of Allergy and
    Infectious Diseases, 58–59, 70,
    75
National Institute of Health, 55, 61,
    77–78
National Veterinary Sciences
    Laboratories, 29
Nebraska, 80
New England Journal of Medicine,
    9–10, 49–50
New Jersey, 17, 80
New York (state), 17, 80
New York City outbreak (1999), 17
    bird deaths and, 9–10
    diagnosis during, 26

overreaction to mosquito bites
during, 51–52
tests on patients during, 8–9
water factor and, 34
Nile River, 16
North Carolina, 80
North Dakota, 80
Novello, Antonia C., 81
nutritional state, 20–21

occupational therapy, 65
Ochlerotatus canadensis (mosquito
species), 39
Ochlerotatus japonicus (mosquito
species), 39
Ohio, 18, 80
Oklahoma, 80
organ transplants, 39–40, 53
oviposition traps (mosquito), 37

Pasteur Institute (Paris), 19, 64
patients. *See* infected people
Pennsylvania, 80
permethrin, 51
pesticides, 77
Petersen, Lyle R., 69, 73
physical therapy, 65
plasmapheresis treatments, 66
Pletnev, Alexander, 77–78
polymerase chain reaction, 46
population growth, 34
prevention
drug treatments, 77–79
extreme measures are not
necessary for, 51–52
goals of, 57
insect repellents, 49–51
laboratory precautions, 55–57
mosquito control, 47–49, 52, 54
preventing mosquito bites, 51,
52–53
public health agencies' guidelines
for, 43, 45
standing water and, 52
surveillance efforts, 45–47
through transfusions and organ
donations, 53–55
propane-generated carbon-dioxide
traps (mosquito), 37
public awareness, 10–12
public health departments, 43, 55

rabbits, 18
raccoons, 18
rainfall fluctuations, 35
research

areas of, 70–71
on drugs to treat West Nile virus,
59, 61–63
on first isolation of West Nile
virus, 15
on genetics, 19–20
on how West Nile virus causes
illness, 74–75
on identification of species of
mosquitoes, 36–39
on methods for destroying
mosquitoes, 73–74
on migrating birds, 73
on preventive drugs, 77–79
on source of West Nile virus,
8–10
specialists for, 71
surveillance of birds and
mosquitoes, 45–47
on transmission of West Nile virus,
29, 72
on West Nile virus outbreak in
Middle East and Africa, 16
Rhode Island, 80
ribavirin, 58, 60
rivers, 34
RNA (ribonucleic acid), 14, 16, 28
rodents, 18
Roehrig, John T., 73
Romania, 17, 29, 34, 35–36
Russia, 17, 34

scientific investigations. *See* research
skunks, 18
South Africa, 35
South Carolina, 80
South Dakota, 80
speech therapy, 65–66
spinal tap, 24
standing water, 35, 51, 52, 54
St. Louis encephalitis virus, 9, 16, 75
supportive therapy, 64
surveillance of birds and mosquitoes,
45–47
symptoms
Guillain-Barré syndrome, 22–23
infected people not showing, 21
variations in severity of, 18–21
West Nile encephalitis, 21–22, 23
West Nile fever, 21, 22

TaqMan assay, 75–76
temperature fluctuations, 35
Tennessee, 80
terrorism, biological, 79, 81
tests, diagnostic, 23–24, 75–76

Texas, 80
transmission
  blood transfusions, 39
  casual contact, 42
  cycle of, 32
  environmental factors increasing,
    34–36
  laboratory contamination, 40–42
  organ transplants, 39–40
  research on, 70, 72–73
  role of birds in, 29–30, 31
  role of mosquitoes in, 30–32
  species of mosquito as factor in,
    36, 38–39
  worldwide, 29
traps. *See specific traps*
treatment
  drug
    clinical trials for, 61–63
    interferon, 58, 60
    laboratory tests, 59, 61
    lack of effective, 58–59
    research on preventive, 77–79
    ribavirin, 58, 60
  supportive therapy, 64–66
trypsin modulating oostatic factor
  (TMOF), 74
Tyler, K.L., 10

Uganda, 15, 16
United States
  Lineage One West Nile virus
    in, 29
  spread of West Nile virus in,
    17–18
  state-by-state prevalence of, 80
University of California, Davis, 38

vaccines, 77–79
vector, the, 32
Vermont, 80
Virginia, 80
viruses
  arboviruses, 16, 17
  classification of, 14
  defined, 13
  entrance of, into cells, 13–14

see also West Nile virus

Washington University School of
  Medicine (St. Louis, Missouri),
  74
water
  rainfall, 35
  in rivers, 34
  standing, 35, 51, 52
West Nile encephalitis, 21–23, 64–65
West Nile meningitis, 21, 23, 64
West Nile meningoencephalitis, 21,
  23, 64
West Nile province (Uganda), 15, 16
West Nile virus
  classification of, 14, 16
  diagnosing, 24–26, 75–77
    differentiating between
      subtypes of West Nile virus,
      25–26
    research on new methods for,
      75–77
    tools and tests, 24–25
  first identification of, 15, 16
  major lineages, 28, 29
  outbreaks
    public awareness and, 10–12
    Romania (1996), 35
    since identification of virus,
      16–18
    South Africa (1974), 35
    see also New York City (1999)
      outbreak
  potency in strains of, 21
  prioritizing battle against, 81
  recovery from, 66–69
  sources of, 8–10
  tracking, 20
  world distribution of, 28
  see also prevention; transmission;
    treatment
West Virginia, 80
wild birds, 9–10
Wisconsin, 80
Wyoming, 80

yellow fever virus, 75

Picture Credits

About the Author

Melissa Abramovitz grew up in San Diego, California, and developed an interest in medical topics as a teenager. She began college with the intention of becoming a doctor but later switched majors and graduated summa cum laude from the University of California, San Diego, with a degree in psychology in 1976.

She launched her career as a freelance writer in 1986 to allow her to be an at-home mom when her two children were small, realized she had found her niche, and continues to write regularly for a variety of magazines and educational book publishers. In her seventeen years as a freelancer she has published hundreds of nonfiction articles and numerous short stories, poems, and books for children, teens, and adults. Many of her works are on medical topics.

At present, she lives in San Luis Obispo, California, with her husband, two college-aged sons, and two dogs.